Contents

Acknowledgements

To my family, I am the lucky one to have all of you in my life. To my teachers and instructors who have guided me over the years, you have helped me develop not only a love and passion for firearms and self-defense, but more importantly you have all played a role in motivating me to become a teacher as well. To my past, current, and future students, thank you all for being a part of this awe-inspiring journey. You are without question the reason I love to teach and why I continue to be so excited about what the future holds. Thank you all for sharing this experience with me and I can't wait to train with all of you!

Fundamental Handgun *Mastery*

Tyson Kilbey

Top Firearms Instruction

Foreword by Rebecca Schmoe

1MMAGC

Tyson Kilbey

Visit my website at
http://www.topfirearmsinstruction.com/

Printed in the United States of America

ISBN-13: 978-1986884730

ISBN-10: 1986884732

Introduction

Writing a book, as I am now completely aware, is a challenging undertaking. But, when you just happen to be writing a book about topics that you love and passionately care about, the "work" involved is worth every laborious minute. When you get to see and share the finished product, the feeling is virtually indescribable!

Over the last several years, I have had amazing, unique, and at times humbling opportunities to train with, learn from, and shoot side by side with some of the best shooters, fighters, and instructors in the world. I have been given the opportunity to develop my skills both in competition and as a teacher. I have trained thousands of law enforcement officers of varying skill levels and stages in their career and thousands of civilian students of varying backgrounds, skill and experience levels, and from nearly all walks of life. Across the Midwest, I have been blessed to have had doctors, lawyers, politicians, media personalities, business owners of all types, and everything in between take part in my courses. I have gotten to train students who had never touched a gun before meeting me, to students who had spent the majority of their lives around firearms. Nearly every single one of them has heard me utter the following words: There are no bad students, only bad teachers. If any part of the training experience was not enjoyable or productive it was always my fault and not theirs. I am holding myself to the same standard for this book. If this book does not motivate you, inform you, and assist you in your quest for knowledge and self-improvement, it is my fault and not yours!

It has been an amazing journey, and although it continues today, I decided that the lessons and concepts I have learned through the various courses and teaching experiences I have had contain the ability to educate and improve the experiences of others. Because of that, the idea for this book originated. When you truly love a topic, it is very common to feel compelled to give back to others so that they may experience the same love, joy, and powerful lessons that you have been fortunate enough to have had.

Rather than being an instructional guide, its design and purpose is to move you forward conceptually in your understanding of handgun mastery. Whether you are a beginner, a hobbyist, or a lifelong gun enthusiast, there are concepts in this book for you.

My friend Rebecca Schmoe will get us started, then I will begin the journey with the most important chapter of all! Enjoy.

Foreword

Dear reader, you have chosen the book,
Fundamental Handgun Mastery. I can surmise a few things
about you simply by the fact that you are reading this
foreword. First of all, I can tell that you are interested
in learning more about how to be a safer and more
proficient, tactically defense minded, handgun operator.
Secondly, it shows me that you value knowledge which can
only come from a life dedicated to extensive research and
range time. Thirdly, by seeking out this book, I can tell
that you are someone who values our inalienable right, which
is enumerated within our United States Constitution, to
protect ourselves with the most effective and efficient
tools available to us. Finally, it is safe to say that you
are someone who is interested in details; all of the
who's, how's, and why's behind the topic at hand. I
can assure you, you've come to the right place.

Prepare yourself for the information
adventure you have been searching for as Tyson
eloquently
and energetically breaks down all of the dynamics
of handgun
ownership and operation. Whether you've never
seen a
handgun in person, you are interested in increased
safety
measures, you are invested in the daily
manipulation and
care of your handgun, you are one of those who are
looking
to improve your tactical defense methods in a
raging gun
battle, or you fall into any expertise level in
between,
there is something in this book for you.

I originally met Tyson when he
promoted his first ever Kids Handgun Safety
Course through
Top Firearms Instruction. As a board member and
blogger for
the national organization 1 Million Moms Against
Gun
Control, I am constantly seeking out safety and
proficiency
courses to share with our followers and associates
across
the country. I happened to notice that his course was
within

driving distance. I contacted him about attending the course
in my capacity as the 1MMAGC SpokesMom and blogger. He
readily accepted, and as you will read in Chapter 2, Teaching Kids Handguns Safety, the rest is history.

By now, I know that you are anxious to
dive in and soak up all of the field tested, and consequently 1MMAGC Mom approved, information awaiting you
in this book. Yet, there is one more thing you should know
before you start on this journey with Tyson. You are the
backbone of the United States of America, dear reader. You
are the protectors of freedom in our land. You, who go above
and beyond, in your quest for knowledge about the tools and
skills which are encompassed within the scope of our second
amendment protected right to defend ourselves, are what
continues to keep our liberty at hand and tyranny at bay. No
matter your personal level of expertise in the realm of
handgun mastery, your dedication to increasing your
knowledge, as well as maintaining your right to exercise

that knowledge, ensures that we will enjoy these freedoms
for generations to come. For that, I wholeheartedly thank
you.
Keep up the good fight!

Yours in freedom,
Rebecca Schmoe
1MMAGC SpokesMom
1mmagc.org
#prepared2protect

Chapter 1 – Safety

Safety is an important consideration in any endeavor. If you play nearly any type of competitive sport, chances are you wear protective equipment. When you are driving, not only should you be wearing a seatbelt, but very likely the vehicle is equipped with airbags. When you are in a public building, it is equipped with fire extinguishers and smoke detectors. The list goes on and on, and of course it only makes sense. If you get injured doing something, you can no longer enjoy it, or do it as effectively as you once could for some period of time.

When it comes to the topic of firearms, safety rises to the highest level of importance. This book will explore several topics related to the fundamentals of handgun use, the mindset and awareness level required to win deadly force engagements, strategies to gain a tactical advantage in a self-defense situation, ways to effectively train for maximum results, and thoughts about the aftermath of a lethal force encounter. But there is no coincidence that the first chapter of this book will be dedicated entirely to the topic of firearm safety. I would not have it any other way. But even after this first chapter, the principles of firearm safety will permeate throughout the book regardless of what particular section we are in. When it comes to firearms, this is a must and there is no room for negotiation.

Why is safety so important when it comes to firearms? Part of the answer is obvious. A mistake in the realm of safety or one moment of carelessness could lead to death. A mistake that can never be corrected. It could be an unintentional discharge of the weapon that leads to the death of the person manipulating the weapon, or someone in the room with or near that person. In either case, a life is unintentionally lost forever. This is unacceptable. When a person dies, the lasting effect ripples through hundreds if not thousands of other people who will be tragically affected because of the loss. In the case where one person accidentally kills another through an unintentional discharge of a weapon, the person who made the mistake will live with that mistake forever and will never fully recover.

There is another aspect of the importance of safety that is not quite as readily apparent. One unintentional discharge of a firearm that injures or kills another person has an adverse effect on every legal and responsible firearm owner in the country. There exists a group of people who want nothing more than to annihilate the rights articulated in the second amendment. They would prefer that the legal ownership and carrying of firearms be completely eliminated. This would be a tragic mistake for more reasons than I have time to cover in this book, but these people exist nonetheless. Every time a firearms "accident" occurs, these people gain momentum and favor for their argument. Once again, this is unacceptable.

There are a lot of "rules" associated with firearms safety. If you attend a shooting competition, there will be a safety brief and rules meeting covering all aspects of firearms safety. If you shoot at a public or private range, there will likely be a sign posted with a list of range safety rules. All major firearms organizations operate under a fixed set of safety rules and regulations.

Most major firearms organizations and entities operate under the same standard rules, and many accept the following four rules as the primary or cardinal rules of firearms safety:

Treat all guns as if they are loaded.

Don't point your gun at anything you

aren't willing to shoot.

Keep your finger off the trigger until you are ready to fire.

Be aware of your target, backstop, and beyond.

Every class I teach, every private lesson I conduct, every time I shoot, I review these four rules. If you were to analyze the details of every tragic firearms accident that has occurred in the history of the world, I am confident that you would find a violation of at least one if not all of these four rules. Each independent one is important in its own right; together, they are the most important rules of all time in regard to firearms safety.

Treat all guns as if they are loaded. This is important for a variety of reasons. First, how you handle and manipulate your gun is habit-forming. If you treat an "unloaded" gun in a different way than you treat a gun when you know it's loaded, there is no doubt that at some point you will confuse the two habits you have created. The chance of this increases exponentially under stress. In case there is any doubt, a gunfight would qualify as a stressful situation. Second, humans by nature make mistakes. You may think a gun is unloaded, you may be ninety-nine percent sure it is unloaded, but one distraction or lapse in memory could mean disaster when assuming your gun is unloaded. Finally, every year people have killed themselves, or someone else, with a gun they thought was unloaded. Firearms owners have killed themselves, their children, their spouses, and their friends with "unloaded" firearms. This is unacceptable.

I was giving a firearms safety presentation to a concealed carry class one day, and I explained the importance of treating all guns as if they were loaded in a similar manner as I did in the previous paragraph. During the presentation, I noticed a middle-aged lady in the front row begin to tear up. As her eyes watered, I could tell that the concept I was explaining was affecting her in a very real and visceral way. At the first break, she approached me and said "I apologize for crying when you were explaining that. I lost my dad 5 years ago when he was cleaning a gun he thought was unloaded." For her, this rule is so real that she lives with a constant reminder of it every day of her life. The rule has the face of a victim attached to it. She is not alone. Story after story exists of people who have been severely injured or killed with a gun that was supposed to be unloaded.

Don't point your gun at anything you aren't willing to shoot. At face value, this seems to make a lot of sense. During the act of shooting at a range, most people are pretty good about following this rule. However, after they have completed that particular string of fire, too many people forget that they are holding a handgun. This rules exists at all times, not just during the actual act of firing. The next time you go to a public range, watch how people handle their guns when they are not in the act of shooting. Now, some of them will be meticulous when it comes to safety and will not violate any of the rules. But unfortunately, there will be some who make you cringe. They will shoot their string of fire, then in one fell swoop turn around and point their muzzle unintentionally at everyone at the range. This is a safety issue that must be addressed immediately. A quality range will have an employee monitoring range safety, if not, it is your responsibility to let the range staff know. On the range, everybody is in charge of safety.

Surprisingly enough, another violation of this rule occurs too frequently because the shooter points the muzzle at him or herself. For example, many people point their guns at various parts of their own bodies when returning their gun to their holster. Do a self-assessment and make sure this is absolutely not the case. Another frequent violation of this rule occurs when practicing with a flashlight.

A significant percentage of self-defense shootings occur in less than ideal light conditions, so it is not uncommon to practice shooting with one hand while the other hand manipulates a flashlight. However, it is incredibly easy to lose focus and cross the hand carrying the flashlight in front of the hand carrying the gun. I have seen this on entirely too many occasions.

Probably the easiest way to practice the rule of not pointing your gun at anything you aren't willing to shoot is to visualize a laser that extends in an infinite straight line starting at the tip of your muzzle. Anything that comes into contact with this laser is now in the immediate danger zone and if you are not willing to shoot it, then you must move your gun immediately. This is sometimes called the laser rule and it is absolutely essential when it comes to firearms safety. Some people and organizations will argue that this is the single most important rule of firearms safety. Whether it is or not, they have a pretty compelling argument.

Keep your finger off the trigger until you are ready to fire. This is absolutely critical, and I can say from teaching thousands of students this is probably the most unintentionally violated firearms safety rule of all time. I have absolutely no scientific proof to back this up, but I have come to believe that it is hard-wired into the human brain to immediately put their finger on the trigger the minute they pick up a handgun. I've said it before, and I will say it again, this is unacceptable! The trigger finger should not be on the trigger, in the trigger guard, or directly next to the trigger guard until you are ready to fire. The appropriate place for your trigger finger is resting straight and fully extended on the side of the weapon above the trigger guard. This is sometimes referred to as universal cover mode. Using this method is absolutely one of the best ways to prevent unintentional discharges.

There are three primary reasons why the universal cover mode is so critical in avoiding unintentional discharges. First is because when you are suddenly startled or scared, which is a high probably during a gunfight, you have a tendency to squeeze your fingers. If this happens with your finger already on the trigger but not ready to shoot, the result could be catastrophic. Second, when you trip and fall, which is a high probably during a gunfight, you have a tendency to squeeze your fingers. Finally, in a close quarter fight, which is a high probably during a gunfight, when one hand is squeezing and clinching and fighting, the other hand has a tendency to follow suit.

As previously stated, this is probably the single most violated safety rule amongst beginner, and even some experienced shooters, that must be corrected.

Be aware of your target, backstop, and beyond. This rule has applications both at the range and out in public when carrying for a self-defense situation. At the range, it is critical to know the limitations of your target, the height of your backstop, and what exists beyond it. The reason for this simple. As a shooter, you are responsible for every single round that comes out of the muzzle of your handgun and its final resting spot.

In one real-life example, a teenage boy was shooting his rifle on his grandpa's land near the interstate. He was shooting in a wooded area and thought that his backstop was high enough to stop all rounds that were going towards the interstate. He was incorrect and one of the rounds traveled out of the woods and struck a motorist in the leg on the highway. After several hours of closing down the interstate due to the possibility of the shooting being an intentional act, the truth was discovered. It was a bad situation that obviously could have been much worse. In this case, the victim was injured but did not die.

Another example of where this rule could come into play is when defending your life. Picture the following scenario: You are about to be attacked by a lethal threat. He is fifteen feet away, reaching for a gun, and says, "I'm going to kill you!" You are able to get your gun and you have a shot. As you are about to shoot to defend your life, a school bus with a kindergarten class pulls up directly behind the attacker. Do you take the shot? What if you fire six rounds, five of them hit the target, but one misses past him and hits a student?

Now every independent situation is slightly different and has its own unique variables. The time of day, the location, the weather conditions, the level of training and experience of the shooter, and so on factor in, but the point I'm making is that you are accountable for every round and by being keenly aware of your target, backstop, and beyond at all times you are putting yourself in the best position to avoid hitting something you did not intend to shoot, and in turn dealing with possibly tragic consequences.

As I said, I review these rules every time I shoot. They are not just something to be glossed over so you can say you did a safety "briefing." These are rules to live by and understand and teach others. I started a private lesson once by asking a shooter to tell me the four cardinal rules of firearms safety and he said, "I have been shooting for a long time, I'm a safe shooter." I responded by saying I have also been shooting for a long time, and because of that, I want you to tell me the four rules of firearms safety. He immediately recognized my point and reviewed the rules of firearms safety with me.

I do not have time to recap and analyze every tragic report or horror story of gun safety-related incidents I have ever seen or heard of, but there is no shortage of them. From the police officer who lost his 3- year- old daughter because he left his gun in a bag in the garage within reach of her, to the mother who was shot and killed in a grocery store by her toddler who was able to get her concealed carry gun from her purse while she was shopping, to the older toddler who shot his infant brother in the head after he was able to get a hold of one of his grandfather's guns, to the cop who accidentally killed himself at a party while showing off his gun to his friends, to the dad that killed himself in his van in front of his kids due to an accidental discharge while his wife was inside shopping, the stories are abundant, tragic and unacceptable.

Firearms safety is critical and firearms owners bare the absolute highest level of responsibility in this area. Firearms safety can and must become a way of life. It must become the beginning, middle, and end of all things firearms related. It can happen and it must happen. There is no room for negotiation and anything less is unacceptable.

I remember training in a tactical firearms class with an instructor from Italy. He had an impressive resume and trained with a number of special operations units and had written firearms training articles in major publications. He had an advanced skill set and some unique tactics, but his concern for safety was completely lacking. He did not conduct a safety review, was not concerned with our target, backstop, and beyond, and did not care where the muzzle of his gun was pointed. At one point he even made the comment that sometimes he shoots in the morning, goes to lunch to have a couple of beers, and then shoots in the afternoon.

I called him out on day one. I explained in great detail every egregious safety violation that occurred and told him that it took away any and all positive aspects that could have been taken from the course. He called me a "Safety Nazi" and asked why I thought the four rules of firearms safety were so necessary. I told him that I had taught firearms to hundreds of students at that point in my life, and I was not going to tell the eight-year-old daughter of one of my students that her dad was never coming home again because he died on the range because of a safety violation.

On day two of the class, we conducted a safety review, and followed the four rules of firearm safety. Furthermore, nobody consumed alcohol during lunch in hopes of improving their shot placement. Firearms safety is not optional, it is essential. The more people we reach and train with this message, the better off we all are.

One night early in my shift as a patrol sergeant, one of the deputies announced on the radio that he might have just been shot at. Several of us responded and met near the location and came up with a game plan. The deputy said he was sitting at a stop sign when he heard the shot. He said his first reaction was to punch the accelerator and get as far away as he could. His adrenaline was up and it seemed like a surreal experience to him. But he was able to pinpoint an area of about three houses that the shot likely came from.

We carefully approached the residences and could hear several people inside of one particular residence near where the deputy was stopped when he heard the shot. We could hear people inside so we decided to make contact. The first gentlemen to answer the door was in his fifties, and he stepped outside and immediately shut the door behind him. I think that it was at that second that I subconsciously knew we were at the house where the shot was fired. We asked him a few basic questions about who was in the house and if he had heard anything suspicious. I could tell he wanted to cooperate with us, and he knew more than what he was telling us. I noticed he mentioned his son at least a couple of times as he answered our questions. Because of this, I asked if his son was there and if I could speak with him. He opened the door and called for his son to come to the outside and speak with us. The second his son came to the door, I now consciously knew I was looking at the person who fired the shot, and I knew it was unintentional. The man was in his early 20's, his face looked flushed, his eyes were wide, his hands were slightly shaking, and you could hear the nervousness in his voice. It didn't take more than three questions for him to admit what happened.

Before we arrived, he was in a back bedroom of the residence showing a couple of his AR-15 rifles he thought were unloaded to a friend of his. He held one rifle, and the friend held another, as they were both looking at them. Then they switched rifles and that's when it happened. He accidentally pulled the trigger and shot a round through the wall. He said his heart started racing because his first thought was that he shot his neighbor. After running next door to check on him, he felt some sense of relief but was still shaken up. The round had actually projected through the wall and past the deputy that was stopped at the stop sign. The situation could have been much worse. The round did not strike anyone. An additional detail about this story worth mentioning is that there were several young children also in the residence when the shot was fired. Before we left the young man said to me, "You don't understand, I am the gun guy in my family. I know more about guns than all of my friends. I always talk about gun safety." How many of the cardinal rules of firearms safety were violated during this incident? Does it matter if you are safe ninety-nine percent of the time but you let up one percent of the time?

The previous story was not an attempt to insult people who say they are "gun guys." It was meant to drive home the point that when it comes to firearms safety it is a one hundred percent all-in proposition and it cannot be any other way. Be the Safety Nazi. After one hundred thousand rounds of experience, I start every shooting day with a review of the four rules of firearms safety. Think safety, live safety, teach safety. It matters.

Now that I have explained and given examples of the importance of the four most important rules, I think there are other safety considerations worth mentioning before we proceed.

First, every time you shoot, everyone in the shooting area should wear both eye and ear protection. No exceptions. Too many people when shooting recreationally go without one or both of these important safety devices.

Consider wearing a billed cap while shooting. When shooting a semi-automatic pistol it is not unheard of for the brass casing to eject back toward the shooter's face. There have been times when the casing has flown back and lodged itself between the shooter's eye and safety glasses.

With the previous tip in mind, it is generally smarter to wear tighter, more form-fitting clothing while shooting at the range. First, this reduces the risk of clothing interfering with your manipulation of the weapon. Furthermore, it is not uncommon for hot brass to eject from the gun and land down the shooter's shirt. This is generally a comical experience for those watching; however, a somewhat painful experience for the shooter. Of more concern is the fact that the shooter generally does a dance consisting of wild and erratic movements to get the round to fall out of their clothes. This in and of itself is not bad; however, it can be extremely problematic if the shooter is still holding his or her gun. If you ever fall victim to hot brass falling into your shirt, remember to holster or lay your gun on the table immediately. Only once that is done, are you free to do the hot brass dance on the range.

When you are on the range, and you drop something, let it fall to the ground. This is difficult to do. The very first instinct we have when we drop something is to try to grab it. Unfortunately, this exactly what a cop did while shooting his 40 caliber handgun on a range near the east coast. After he dropped his gun, he attempted to catch it before it hit the ground. During the fall, the muzzle turned toward him and as he squeezed to catch it he pressed the trigger with fatal results. With most properly functioning handguns, you are far better off allowing it to drop instead of trying to catch it.

Finally, have a game plan in case of an emergency. Do you know the location of the nearest hospital? Do you have a first aid kit? Do you have access to a device that can be used as a tourniquet in case someone his shot in a limb area? Coming up with a brief game plan in case of an emergency will undoubtedly prepare you, and everyone at the range, in case of an emergency.

I hope that this chapter has set the stage for the rest of this book, and the rest of your firearms career. If you were to draw literally nothing else from this book but a renewed appreciation for the importance of firearms safety, than that in itself is a win. But of course I do not think that is the case or else I would stop now. But it is important to understand that the principles and tenets of firearms safety will remain in effect from now on as we explore the ways to gain the tactical advantage when carrying concealed. The path to true handgun mastery is built on a solid foundation of firearms safety!

Chapter 2 – Teaching Kids Handguns Safety

I almost did not finish writing Fundamental Handgun Mastery because of this chapter. Not because I did not like the direction or purpose of the book. Also not because it was not important or completely necessary. I almost put everything on hold to write an entire book about the topic of this very chapter! Teaching children firearms safety is not only important, but I would say understanding the principles that I will layout in this chapter are absolutely essential to everyone's journey to firearms mastery.

Of all the firearms and self-defense courses I have taught in the last decade, at all of the locations, with all of the students both civilian and law enforcement, there is one course that I am not only most proud of, but that has been more popular than all of the rest of them combined. That course is Kids Handgun Safety!

Since that course was created, I have had the

tremendous pleasure of teaching it in multiple locations with exceptional feedback from students, parents, teachers, and firearms instructors alike. Law enforcement agencies have contacted me to observe and assist in the course so they can implement their own programs, and numerous news agencies and media outlets have reported on the course and its purpose.

I have sometimes wondered why this course, in particular, has been so successful and popular. But when I think about it, there is really no surprise. The course is popular for a number of reasons. First, teaching children firearm safety is imperative and will positively save lives and subsequently, everyone can benefit from it. Next, the methodology I have chosen to employ to teach children this important topic is fun, high-energy, and most importantly memorable. Finally, make no mistake, when I teach children firearms safety, I am also teaching their parents and guardians.

The first time I ever taught a Kids Handgun Safety Course was really just a spur of the moment decision. I remember I was teaching a concealed carry course that weekend and in the free moments of the weekend, I thought why not do a small kids handgun safety course? I decided I would give the children a brief game plan on what to do if they or any other children they were playing with ever saw an unsecured gun of any type in any location. We talked through examples and scenarios and we discussed a typical four-step operation that many entities and organizations use. It boils down to this process: Stop, do not touch the gun, get away from that area, and report it to a parent or trusted adult. After we developed, reviewed, and committed the game plan to memory, we talked about shooting all types of guns under the direct supervision of a parent or guardian or an approved instructor. The four cardinal rules of safety were discussed, demonstrated, and practiced with the use of plastic guns. During the course, we played games like Simon Says, Four Corners, and for the Grand finale: Dodgeball! It was fun, high-energy, and unbeknownst to me at the time, the beginning of something big.

In attendance at that first Kids Handgun Safety Course was a member of One Million Moms Against Gun Control who was very active in gun-related issues and a prolific blogger. She wrote a brief blog entry about the event which was the following:

Education and Empowerment; Protecting Future Generations from Misinformation

A group of eight children, ranging in age from preschool to seventh grade, watch a short film that lays out the four basic gun safety rules for children. Their parents, in an adjoining room, are being commended on taking competent and necessary steps to prevent gun-related tragedies.

Instructor, Tyson Kilbey, takes a moment to reiterate to the parents that pretending like guns are not around does not prevent accidental gun injuries and deaths. Telling a child to never touch a gun only adds to the mystery and curiosity which leads to unsafe handling of firearms. He takes is a step further and urges parents to, "make gun training a constant process. Make it fun, and they will continue to practice safe gun handling their entire lives."

After the children introduce

themselves the room quickly fills with laughter as Kilbey leads them in a high energy game of Simon Says. Kilbey has all of the children's direct and active attention on him. They listen to every word and hurriedly obey. The children are having a blast as he is effortlessly establishing authority in the room.

Once the final child obeys the last command and the game has been won, instructor David Whisenhunt steps in to reiterate the lessons learned from Eddie Eagle. The children, excited to share their knowledge, shout out the four rules for children and guns.

1) Stop
2) Don't touch
3) Leave the area
4) Tell a trusted adult

Whisenhunt then stretches their mode of thinking, as they prepare to move into the four cardinal rules of gun safety, by asking, "How do you know if a gun is loaded?" To which one boy quickly replies,

"You don't. That's why you don't touch it."
Kilbey steps up and writes the numbers one
through four on the whiteboard and asks
the group to explain the rules for safe gun
handling. Obviously, some of the children
had heard these before as hands raise,
thrashing the air around them, voices
shouting, "Pick me! I know! Treat all guns
as if they are loaded!"

"Never point a gun at anything you
are not willing to shoot."

"Know your target and what's
behind it."

"Keep your finger off the trigger
until you are ready to shoot."

Kilbey points out there is one more
rule and Whisenhunt steps in to reiterate
that you can't tell if a gun is unloaded
simply by looking at it. One of the children
blurts out that, "there could still be a bullet
in the chamber" even if the magazine is

out, to which Kilbey demonstrates with the use of dummy ammunition.

Both instructors form a line and use training guns (blue guns) to teach the children the importance of keeping your finger off the trigger and never pointing a gun at anything you are not willing to shoot.

During the training, one little boy is heard saying to a friend, "Don't point that at me, I like my life!"

Soon, all of the children feel comfortable and their curiosity has been quelled, the room once again erupts in games and laughter as they play they are reminded gently about thinking things through and being aware and responsible for the safety of themselves and those around them.

After the last game is over, the children review what they have learned. A five-year-old girl, who had started the class reluctant and shy, was beaming with pride as she recited, "Stop, don't touch, leave, get a grownup!" (Though I honestly think her dad, who was looking on, was even more proud of her than she could possibly be of herself.)

Each child was called up and presented with a certificate of training and given a few pieces of candy for their hard work."

When asked, one mom explained that, "with more friends and family owning guns, I want my child to know what to do around them. I can't be there to protect my child in every situation, but I can teach them ways to protect themselves." Then a dad chimed in offering, "If you're a parent you know that sometimes your kids don't listen to you. But, sometimes they are more likely to listen to someone else who says the exact same thing as you. So you have to find someone you trust and I wouldn't trust anyone but Kilbey and Whisenhunt to train my kids." This statement was met with resounding agreement from all the parents in the room.

In no time, the small voices and high energy that had filled the room moments before, were all headed on their way to family and activities that were awaiting them. Yet, it's satisfying to know that those eight children now know the basics of gun safety. Even more, it's encouraging to know that those children can help educate those in their sphere of influence, both peers as well as adults.

A special thank you to Tyson Kilbey and David Whisenhunt, with Top Firearms Instruction, for giving me the opportunity to observe the Kids Handgun Safety Course.

Keep up the good fight!

Rebecca Schmoe

The event was an absolute blast. Overall, it appeared that it was just another normal weekend of teaching firearms and self-defense to great groups of students. Monday morning came along, and I got an email from the Administrative Assistant for the Sheriff of Johnson County at the time. She told me the Sheriff would like to speak with me in his office.

Now, the vast majority of people who hear that the big boss wants to see them in his office will go through a very distinct process. They will begin playing back every single interaction and experience in their past to find out exactly at what point they messed up to find themselves in their current situation. I must admit that although I could not think of anything I had done, I was a bit concerned that the visit with the Sheriff was not going to be a pleasant one. I was wrong.

To my surprise and excitement, the Sheriff had called me into his office because he saw the Kids Handgun Safety Course on social media and he asked me if I would lead more courses for his agency. I was ecstatic at the idea, and a few months later the first course was put out to the general public. In less than twenty-four hours, the first course had all twenty spots reserved. So we put on another course and expanded the course to thirty kids. It too filled up in less than twenty-four hours.

It had become very clear that there was a strong, yet largely unfulfilled need for quality and meaningful training for children in the area of firearms safety. And I am gleamingly proud to say that even to the date of this writing, the Kids Handgun Safety Course is going strong and continues to grow in support and reach more and more members of the community.

Throughout the years' parents, grandparents, teachers, etc. have asked me about teaching firearms safety to kids. Common themes, questions, and statements are made during these interactions. "At what age should I teach kids about guns? If I teach kids about guns how do I know they won't use them improperly? What kind of guns should a child be able to shoot? I never grew up with guns in the house so I just keep my kids away from guns to keep them safe. I like guns but my wife is scared of them." As I said, the same themes, questions, concerns, and problems are very commonly brought up by concerned adults.

I usually start my explanation of teaching gun safety to children the following way: Imagine you put a can of soda on top of a table. Then you told an eight-year-old boy who is in the room with you, "Do not ever drink from this magical can of mystery, you got it?" What do you think he is going to do as soon as you leave the room? Yes, he is going to chug that thing to the bottom as fast as he can! Curiosity is a natural emotion for most people, and quadruple that when you are talking about children. The reality is kids want to learn about guns. Kids are naturally curious about guns. One way or another they are going to learn about guns. The question is who is going to teach them and is what they learn going to be safe, useful and correct? With the hundreds of thousands of guns in this country and the countless ways you can be unsafe with them, this is not a subject that should be approached without the correct strategy. Furthermore, not teaching them anything about guns at all is not an effective approach.

Now take the scenario in the last paragraph and change it up. "This is a soda. It is not healthy for you but it does have a sweet taste. You are allowed to try it, in moderation after a healthy dinner." This approach, unlike the first, is much less likely to result in him "chugging" the soda behind your back.

What age is appropriate to teach children about gun safety? AS SOON AS POSSIBLE. There is no reason why a three-year-old cannot be taught to Stop, Don't Touch, Leave, and Tell an Adult. Giving children a plan beyond "just keeping guns away from them" is critical. And it can and will save lives.

What is the right age for a child to actually

shoot a gun? I also think the answer to this is much younger than people realize. It is important that dry fire practice (physically practicing without live ammunition---explained in greater detail later in this book) be done a substantial amount prior to the actual live shooting of the weapon. At the age of say seven or eight, using an extremely low recoil gun such as a .22 is a perfect starting point.

To close out the chapter I would like to share a little more about the philosophy and methodology of teaching firearms safety and fundamentals to children. ONE training session is NOT enough! Every skill, knowledge set, or learned ability is perishable to some extent. If I were your child's soccer coach and I told you we were going to have one practice in which I teach them how to kick the ball, pass the ball, and the rules of the game, and from then on we will not practice anymore—we would probably lose every game. But consistent, focused practice on the other hand, leads to incredible results. In the area of firearms safety and fundamentals, there is no room for shortcuts.

But how do you motivate people to train consistently? In my opinion, the answer is simple. Make it fun. Some instructors insist that training should not be fun. I disagree. I look forward to training every day of my life. Training is not stressful it is fun. The results of this mindset are undeniable. This is worth repeating---make training fun. With children the bottom line is to teach them to be safe, praise their efforts, and give them credit because they are picking up more than you realize. Know and understand that consistent, focused practice does, in fact, lead to the desired result and often times exceeds your expectations.

I firmly, passionately, and without question believe that teaching and training children of all ages firearms safety is a positive, powerful, and possibly life-saving endeavor. Ultimately, when you train the younger generation you are also training yourself. It truly is a situation where everyone wins.

Chapter 3 – Tools and Gear

Of all the questions students have asked me in Concealed Carry Classes and Handgun Seminars, I would say eighty percent of them have to do with what I will address in this chapter. What kind of gun is the best for concealed carry? What kind of ammunition should I use? What do you think about holsters? Should I carry an extra magazine? What is the best way to store a handgun? How often do I need to clean my gun? Should I lighten the trigger pull for better results? Should I get a laser sight? What about night sights? All of these are legitimate questions, and I will address my thoughts and opinions in several of these areas throughout this section. But before I do, I should give the warning that I rarely if ever give a specific answer to questions like these. I don't think there is a perfect way. I don't think there is a perfect gun or a perfect piece of equipment. Furthermore, even if there was, over time something would evolve and become better. Add to that the fact that what works for you, might not work for me. We all have different strengths and weaknesses, different body types, levels of strength and flexibility, and so forth. All of this comes into consideration when choosing gear and equipment. In addition, while the gear you use is not completely irrelevant when it comes to gaining the tactical advantage when carrying concealed, it is not nearly as important as the proper mindset, awareness, and commitment to training. All of which will be addressed in future chapters.

What is the best gun to carry? The one that will save your life. That is usually my response when someone asks me that question. Of course, I do not just leave it at that, but the answer I give does explain more than it appears to. The reality is choosing a concealed carry gun is not just as simple as looking at someone and saying, "You look like a Smith & Wesson guy!" or "Yep, you are definitely a Glock girl!"

I personally carry a Glock Model 43. It is a compact 9mm handgun. It is the one that I believe will save my life or someone else's life if the extremely unfortunate circumstance arises. I choose Glock not because I think it is the greatest gun in the universe, but because it is the gun that I shoot exponentially more than any other type of gun. It feels comfortable when I shoot it and carry it. It is an incredibly resilient weapon, and when I shoot it, I hit my target.

Some people expect some secret, magic formula in determining which gun is the best for them to carry. The reality is when it comes to firearms I really boil it down to two questions. Is what I am doing simple? Does what I am doing make sense? If I can answer yes to both of those questions, then more often than not I have found the correct answer.

So if one of my students asks me that question, this is the road map I give them. Try some different guns. Do you like how it feels when you shoot it? Are you able to shoot it with an acceptable degree of accuracy? If you answered yes to those questions you are well on your way to finding your gun.

I should note that one firearms instructor I have had in the past made the comment that the way to choose a concealed carry handgun is to pick the biggest gun that you are willing to carry. He would follow that up by stating that he had never heard of anyone in a gunfight wishing they had a smaller gun. While it's kind of humorous, there is some truth to that statement. While it's not exactly my preferred method of choosing a gun, I do share that line with my students on a frequent basis because I think it follows the method of simplicity and common sense.

In some sense, I may be oversimplifying things,

but when it comes to firearms too many people have a tendency to overanalyze things. They buy a dozen different "tactical" modifications for their gun so that it is ninjafied to the tenth degree. But even when they're done, they can still barely shoot it. Even worse still, it is way too uncomfortable to actually carry.

There are definitely some additional basic factors to keep in mind when choosing the best gun for you. Do you want to carry a semi-automatic pistol or a revolver? There are definitely advantages and disadvantages associated with each one. A quality revolver is extremely dependable. And in the rare case that the gun does go "click" instead of "bang" your immediate remedy is simply to press the trigger again. A quality semi-automatic handgun can also be reliable and in the event you need more ammunition, reloading a second magazine is fairly easy. However, if a semi-automatic gun goes "click" instead of "bang" the process to correct the malfunction may take more time. More on this later. There are positives and negatives with everything, so knowing what they are and what works better for you is the key to resolving those issues.

Students have asked me if it is advisable to choose a couple of different guns for concealed carry. My response is usually one of caution. For example, would it make sense to carry a gun like a

Glock with no external safety mechanism on some occasions, and then to carry a gun that has a manually manipulated safety mechanism other times? I would say no. Under the stress of a lethal force encounter, the likelihood of confusing the two would be too great. I remember a former trainer of mine said he experienced a similar situation years earlier when he held a suspect at gunpoint with the external safety engaged unknowingly. This was an experienced law enforcement officer and trainer whose agency had recently switched gun models. The event ended without incident, but had he been forced to shoot to save his life or someone else's, the result could have been tragic.

What about carrying two guns concealed? Are there advantages to this? Well if the time came that you needed a second gun because of a malfunction, your attacker disarmed you, or you were out of ammunition, then you would be thrilled to have the second gun. On the other hand, how much time are you willing to spend strapping handguns and holsters to various locations of your body prior to going out shopping?

Inevitably, a conversation about gun types will at some point lead to ammunition type and caliber. Again at the risk of oversimplifying things, there are some basic considerations and positives and negatives to consider.

Some people will swear by .40 or .45 caliber ammunition because anything smaller will not have the stopping power they need. Some people choose 9mm or .380 because they do not feel like they can control the recoil of a larger round.

I choose 9mm hollow point ammunition from a reputable company. The reason I choose 9mm ammunition is because I know from actual incidents that it does have threat stopping power, it has less recoil than larger rounds, and it is cost-efficient. I practice with ball ammunition, but I carry hollow-point ammunition. The advantage of hollow point ammunition is that it has a tendency to expand upon contact with human flesh, and in the event of a missed target has less tendency to ricochet than ball ammunition. This is a win-win situation. I should note that it is critical to shoot at least a few hundred rounds of the ammunition you want to carry through your concealed carry gun to make sure it functions properly and you are confident with it. Obviously, the topic of ballistics and ammunition selection is extremely vast and there are a lot of additional factors that one could consider, but once again the system I use has worked for me and many others and has been validated by a good friend of mine who has years of experience as a forensic firearms examiner and has probably seen more ammunition demos than there are words in this book. So I would say my decision is simple and it makes sense.

Holster selection is definitely an important consideration when choosing to carry concealed. I have actually been asked if a holster is even necessary at all. My answer is yes. Simply putting a gun in your pocket is not a good idea. Aside from the difficulty in drawing the weapon that it creates, the chance of an unintentional discharge during the draw also increases.

There are a lot of different brands and types of holsters. There are ankle holsters, appendix carry holsters, strong side inside the pant holsters, cross draw holsters, underwear holsters, small of the back holsters and many more. There are all sorts of materials that holsters are made of to include leather, kydex, and felt materials. Applying the same formula that I always do to firearms-related questions, I have come up with a system that works well for me. I carry an inside the pant strong side holster made of kydex material. It is custom fit to my Glock 43. The holster itself completely covers the trigger guard of the weapon, and the weapon fits securely enough in the holster that if I were to turn it upside down the gun will not fall out of the holster. The reason I chose the strong side inside the pant location is because it is easily concealable, relatively comfortable, and the overwhelming majority of my gun draws come from that location anyway, so it makes complete sense to keep my gun in that location.

Whatever you chose as your holster type, and whatever location you chose to carry, it should be a location that you are comfortable with carrying (or else you won't carry your weapon), and it should be a location that you can and will practice drawing from. Furthermore, it is a wise investment to spend some money on a quality holster. If you buy a fifteen dollar holster, expect a fifteen dollar value. A quality holster for concealed carry generally costs anywhere from sixty to eight dollars.

Locations that may seem to make sense or look cool, may not be as realistic or reliable as you initially think. Of the people I know who have worn ankle holsters, most of them do not like them. If there is any type of running or fighting involved, the chance of the gun or holster coming loose and moving or shifting locations is great. In addition, the ability to draw from the ankle is somewhat dependent on environment (It would be difficult to draw from inside a vehicle for example). So, unless you can quickly ninja roll to a position of advantage, an ankle holster is probably not the best option for a primary weapon.

Cross-draw shoulder holsters may have

looked cool in old detective movies, but in reality, they are pretty uncomfortable and not incredibly easy to draw from. Small of the back holsters fall into that same category for me. Try spending time in a seated position, or in a vehicle, with a gun holstered in the small of your back. Some people like appendix holsters, and from a vehicle or seated position they are probably the easiest to draw from. For some people, placing a gun that close to the center of their pelvis is not an appealing proposition.

One other important consideration when it comes to holsters that I should mention is its level of retention. Meaning, how securely is it fit into the holster? On one end, you can get a high-level super retention holster that requires four independent release mechanisms and an audible passcode requirement (this is a joke, please do not try to search for this, even in California) and on the other end is a holster that simply wraps around the gun with no type of retention device whatsoever. In my opinion, it is wise to have some type of retention device due to the possibility that the self-defense situation becomes a close quarter battle in which you risk the possibility of being disarmed and killed with your own gun. But, the retention should not be so high level that you will have difficulty, or even worse be completely unable to draw your gun, should the need arise. Again, this is a personal decision and there are positives and negatives. Know them and train accordingly. More on this later.

Some females choose to carry concealed in their purse as opposed to using a holster. This is an understandable option, but the following things should be considered. In this case, I would highly encourage the use of a purse specifically designed for concealed carry. A purse like this will likely have a separate compartment with a holster for the handgun. Under no circumstances would I recommend carrying a gun in a purse without a holster. For one thing, everybody knows that women generally carry one of everything known to man in their purses, which would be problematic when they try to draw their gun only to find, lipstick, mirror, shoehorn, and shark repellent first. Furthermore, the chance of an unintentional discharge increases exponentially.

In many of my concealed carry courses and women's self-defense courses students have had strong debates with each other about carrying any type of weapon at all in their purse. Some claim that the first thing a potential mugger will take is your purse, so what use would a weapon have in there? Others reply if they want your purse to throw it and run the other way. No amount of money or property is, or ever will be, worth your life. I love when these discussions evolve in my classes because the reality is there are elements of truth in each of their statements and concerns. Sometimes just by taking part in these discussions, students begin to develop an understanding of what works best for them. There is no perfect way to do things for everyone. Self-defense situations are unique. But without question, discussing and formulating ideas about your personal defense plan will make you safer and more prepared.

I have two final considerations when it comes to carrying concealed in your purse. First, practice drawing from your purse so you can do it confidently under stress. Finally, under no circumstances should you leave your purse anywhere that is not completely and unquestionably under your immediate control. No exceptions.

When you carry your gun, my recommendation is that it should be completely concealed. Be careful not to allow the gun to "print" through your clothes displaying the outline of the gun. I should note that you should always follow the laws in your particular state or jurisdiction with respect to concealed carry, open carry, etc., but ultimately if concealed carry is an option, it is superior to open carry. You do not draw unnecessary attention to yourself when you carry concealed, you do not lose a tactical advantage by letting the "bad guy" know you have a gun, and you run less risk of someone disarming you. Believe it or not, open carry citizens have been robbed for their guns.

Finally, I have to address one of the long-standing debates amongst gun owners. This question definitely comes up often in my concealed carry courses. I have moderated some serious back and forth discussions about this topic. Should you carry a round in the chamber or not? I am not going to answer the question but instead, I am going to throw out some ideas and concepts and leave the ultimate decision up to you. The primary advantages of carrying a round in the chamber are that you have an extra round, and you will be seconds faster to fire in a life and death battle. The primary advantages of leaving the chamber empty are that you have less chance of suffering from an unintentional discharge, and in the event your gun is taken from you, it will take longer for the bad guy to shoot at you. Decide what is best for you, and train accordingly.

Where and how should you store your gun? There are a lot of different opinions about this and I have heard both extremes on this one. There are people who store the gun completely loaded and laying on the pillow next to them at night. Then there are others who store their guns locked out of battery, locked in a storage case, with no ammunition in the same room. The argument for one extreme is to have it immediately available in case of a home invasion. The argument for the other extreme is to make sure it is impossible to access by anyone who should not have it. Both of those are factors to consider. For me, I have chosen a system that is simple and easy. I keep my guns secured, but I can access them quickly if the need arises. Also, EVERY TIME I access my gun, I count it as a training repetition and treat it as such. Accessing my handgun in a life and death situation is of critical importance. Also, keeping my guns secured so that no unauthorized person can ever get to them is of equally critical importance. Because of this, please put careful thought and consideration into the storage of your guns.

Most of my guns are locked and stored at work. However, my Glock 43 is stored in a safe in my bedroom closet. It is pointed in the same direction every time, with an empty chamber and two loaded magazines next to it. The safe is locked and the key is hidden in a location in my bedroom. When I carry my gun, which is everyday incidentally, I obtain the key, open the safe, grip the gun in the same way I do when I shoot, establish a sight picture, insert a magazine into the magazine well, rack the slide which in turn chambers the round, then finish the process by holstering the weapon and attaching it to my belt. Finally, I grab the second magazine and put it into my support side back pocket. Every time. The process takes between twenty-three to twenty-five seconds. This process provides me with a sense of security in that it is safely stored, and accessible in a reasonable amount of time. Furthermore, it provides me a training repetition of retrieving and manipulating my weapon that I believe will pay off over time. This system makes sense and works for me.

Different people will give you different advice on how to store your firearm. My advice is this, you have the ultimate level of responsibility when it comes to your weapons. If anyone, your child, a friend, a neighbor, accesses your weapon, without or without our permission, you bear some level of responsibility. Obviously, if a burglar breaks into your home and steals your gun and you report the crime, this would be an exception, but barring a similar scenario you are liable for the safekeeping and storage of your guns and anything that happens as a result of you not protecting them in the highest regard is something you will be held at least in part accountable for. That being said, it does make sense to store them in such a way that if you needed to access them yourself, you could do it in a reasonable amount of time.

Your particular situation, location, and set up of your house are all relevant factors. Do you have children? Who has access to your house? Is it an apartment? Is it a two-story house? How many guns do you have? Is what you have decided safe and reasonable? It is your responsibility to answer these questions.

The last topic I want to address in this chapter is cleaning, maintenance, and modifications to your weapon. When it comes to cleaning and maintenance of your weapon, the owner's manual is your primary guide. If you do not have a manual for your weapon, nearly every weapon systems manual can be located online. You should be familiar enough with your weapon to be able to break it down to the four or five basic components that allow you to clean it. Breaking down your weapon in this way is oftentimes referred to as a field strip. A Glock, for example, can be disassembled into the slide, frame, barrel, recoil spring assembly, and magazine for cleaning purposes. A certified armorer can disassemble the weapon further, but for standard cleaning and maintenance, this is generally not necessary.

I would recommend following the manufacturer's recommendations for how often you should clean your weapon. For me, it depends on what that particular gun is used for. If it is a practice gun that I do not intend to carry for self-defense, then it is not as critical to clean it every time I shoot it. If it is a gun that I carry on duty or for self-defense, then it only makes sense to clean it every time it is shot.

A dependable, functional gun cleaning kit can be bought in whole or part at most local shopping centers. My recommendation is to buy cleaning materials specifically for gun cleaning. Experimenting with oils and solvents that are not specifically for gun cleaning could be harmful to your weapon. Don't take shortcuts when it comes to cleaning. For example, don't follow the lead of the police officer who thought he would save time by putting his gun in his dishwasher to clean it. His gun may have smelled nice, but other than that, I don't think it achieved its intended result. My final caution about gun cleaning is the following: The most common mistake new and intermediate level shooters make when it comes to cleaning handguns is using too much oil. An extremely small amount of oil is all that is necessary for most semi-automatic handguns. The danger in over oiling your weapon is that dirt and grime will be attracted to the additional oil, which can result in interrupting the cycle of operation of the pistol, causing it to malfunction. This is counterproductive.

If you have been around the gun crowd for any amount of time, you have realized that a lot of us are "gadget guys." We like to add tactical parts to our guns. We like night sights, scopes, lasers, trigger adjustments, mounted flashlights, and whatever other "tactical" gear we can possibly add to our gun. In following with my simple is best mindset, these additions and modifications are not for me. I am not completely against additions. But more importantly, a solid gun straight from the manufacturer, coupled with a desire to train safely and properly is all I believe is necessary. From my time on SWAT to firearms instructor schools, to running drills at the range, it is my experience that the more gear you add the more likely something, or some part, of your equipment will malfunction. As a new SWAT operator, I remember taking five knives, two of each of my less lethal options, and additional ninja gear in every pocket on every operation. By the end of my SWAT career, I only took the bare essentials. The same holds true on the range. I remember one rifle instructor school where on day one most people had more gear than they could carry. By day five, they were down to their rifle and magazines.

This chapter provided direction and ideas pertaining to some of the most common questions about gear, holsters, cleaning, ammunition, and firearms maintenance that students frequently ask. Each topic can and should be researched further on your own. I gave opinions based on my experience; however, your situation may be different and you may have a sound, logical reason for choosing a different path. This is perfectly okay and recommended. But, while good quality, functional equipment is important, it is only one small piece in gaining the tactical advantage along the path to handgun mastery. The proper awareness and mindset, a solid understanding of the fundamentals, and a desire and commitment to improve through training are also critical components that will give you the advantage you might someday need to save a life. So those will be the areas addressed in the following chapters.

Chapter 4 – Awareness and Mindset

In terms of gaining a tactical advantage, this is probably the most important chapter of the book. I have heard experienced shooters say on several occasions that "shooting is ninety percent mental." I would agree. The reality is most things are. The focus of this chapter will be the importance of mindset and awareness in regard to concealed carry, and how you can use a proper awareness level to avoid being in a gunfight altogether. That would be the best-case scenario. I remember a former police firearms instructor used to say, "If I would have known I was going to be in a gunfight today, I would have called in sick for sure." While he obviously made the statement in jest, the underlying theme is you do not want to be in a gunfight.

If anyone chooses to carry concealed because they want to get into a shootout, they are carrying for the wrong reason. If someone is carrying because they want to feel power over others, they are carrying for the wrong reason. I carry concealed virtually every day of my life, and I never want my gun to leave my holster. That being said, if the need arises, I want to be trained to the highest level possible. I want to be physically and mentally prepared to save my life or another innocent life. This is a huge responsibility and although you can never really be sure how you are going to act in a moment of extreme stress, you can prepare yourself to the best of your ability.

I think first you have to believe in the reason why you are carrying. For me, the best articulation I have ever heard on why honest, responsible citizens should carry concealed if they are willing to physically and mentally prepare to do so is laid out in the essay Sheep, Sheepdogs, and Wolves by Lieutenant Colonel Dave Grossman. I recommend anyone who is deciding whether or not they should carry concealed read this essay. It places people into three categories. First, there are the sheep, represented by the vast majority of people who have no capacity for violence or even the thought of violence. Then there are the wolves who prey on the sheep. Finally, there are the sheepdogs who have a capacity for violence but only resort to it when protecting the sheep from wolves. I believe the essay is a brilliant analogy for the existence of people who commit evil acts, the denial by many people that these evil-doers exist, and an explanation of the people who know it is up to them to stand up to these evil people. There is a story of a man who denied this evil, although he could have carried concealed and saved the lives of others. Although not his fault, he bears the guilt of his denial for the rest of his life. This essay gives powerful motivation to the good people of the world who do not want to use violence, but will do it to save innocent lives.

The previous paragraph is one of the reasons I feel so passionately about the importance of concealed carry. I never want to use my weapon against a person. But even more than that, I never want to be in a position where I could have saved the life of a son, a daughter, a wife, a mother, a father, a friend, or for that matter any innocent person, but I couldn't do it because I chose not to carry concealed that day. I see my gun as a lifesaving tool, not a life taking tool. A gun to a concealed carry citizen is like a fire extinguisher to a firefighter. It is like a seatbelt to a race car driver. You never want to have to use it, but you also never want to be in a position where you needed it but didn't have it. Responsible citizens who train and prepare and legally carry concealed are a win for the good guys and loss for the bad guys.

The saying "When seconds count, the police

are minutes away" is unfortunately all too true. This is not always the case, but most of the time it is. The police do not want it to be this way, but this is the nature of crime and how it is reported. Typically, an act of violence occurs. Then, when a victim or witness is able and makes the decision to do so, they call the police. A dispatcher designated as the call taker answers and begins taking down the information about the crime. This call taker then begins giving this information to a second dispatcher who in turn relays the information to the officer in his patrol car. The officer then proceeds to the location of the crime. While all of this is happening, most of the time the suspect is not even at the location where the crime originally occurred.

The saying "The best way to stop a bad guy with a gun, is to have a good guy with a gun" is simple, but oftentimes completely true. This is especially true when dealing with the subject of active killers (sometimes referred to as active shooters). I prefer to use the term "Active killers" because sometimes the weapon of choice for mass murder is not a gun. Active killers are a compelling reason for any responsible able-bodied citizen to carry concealed. This is an evil that most people do not like to talk about, but in this day and age nobody can deny. Spend a few months searching news stories for mass killings and active shooter incidents and you will be amazed by how frequently these events actually occur. These mass killings have occurred in elementary schools, middle schools, high schools, movie theaters, beaches, places of worship, places of business, shopping malls, fast-food restaurants, concerts, night clubs and public streets to name a few. Generally speaking, the carnage doesn't end until it is stopped by armed police or armed citizens. Active killers are a compelling reason for any responsible citizen to carry. As an added note, even if you are not carrying concealed there are specific strategies and methods you can employ to neutralize an active killer. That is not the focus of this particular book, but training citizens in effective responses to active killer incidents has been a major part of the Top Firearms Instruction curriculum for some time, and I expect that trend to continue.

Now that we have established the importance of concealed carry, it is equally important to understand the pivotal role awareness plays in not only preventing you from having to use your gun, but also in giving you the tactical advantage if you do have to use it. If you truly want to be safe, walking around with your "head in the clouds" is simply not an option. I am not saying you should walk around in hyper-vigilant combat mode every time you are in public. This would be mentally exhausting, unnecessary, and counterproductive. But, when in public you should visually scan the area around you. You should be cautious. You should notice people, things, and activities happening around you. You should not ignore your "sixth sense." That feeling that something is not right. Often times this is not some magical mystery sense, but simply your subconscious mind recognizing something out of place before you consciously recognize what it is. There have been several incredible books written on this subject, and I am giving only a brief synopsis of this, but it is critically important.

When I explain this concept to people in my classes, most of them agree and claim that they already do this. They say they are extremely cautious and always aware of things going on around them. But are they really? I think an honest assessment of most people is that even when in public, they spend much of their time oblivious to things going on around them. I usually ask people to spend some time in a public place watching people and then tell me if they disagree. The reality is the vast majority of people are wrapped up in their own worlds, with multiple things going on, and multiple distractions on top of that. From a tactical standpoint, this lack of awareness would put anyone at a major disadvantage.

There is another advantage to actively paying attention to your awareness level. More often than not, bad guys choose their victims. Of course, there are some victims of opportunity, and wrong place, wrong time scenarios, but more often than not, victims are chosen because they look like easy targets. Who is an easier target than someone who is distracted, oblivious, and blissfully unaware of the things going on around them? Although the claims of criminals should be taken with a grain of salt, many convicted felons have confessed that their victims were chosen specifically because they appeared to be unaware, unwilling, or unable to fight back. While it may be difficult to think in terms of a bad guy, who would you pick as your victim to rob? Would you pick someone who appears to be scanning the area around them? Would you choose someone who obviously sees you when you are thirty yards away as opposed to five feet away?

Now that we have established the importance of awareness, we should take it a step further. I mentioned previously the importance of listening to your "sixth sense." I think this is critical, yet difficult to do. In active killer incidents, when you see the news interviews with the witnesses, very rarely do you hear, "I knew right away it was gunshots." On the contrary, you usually hear statements like, "It sounded like fireworks" or "I thought it was a car backfiring." I have come to believe that nearly all people have a tendency to block out evil and worst-case scenarios and try to rationalize what they are seeing or hearing. I have heard this phenomenon actually identified before as Normalcy Bias. In short, the normal functioning human has an exceptionally difficult time mentally processing danger and tragic acts, even when they occur right in front of them. This can be deadly in terms of defending your own or a loved one's life. This denial and rationalization can in turn lead to a complete shutdown and panic paralysis once you finally realize that what you are seeing is a threat. Knowing and realizing that we have a tendency to rationalize and downplay cues of danger is an important step in regaining the tactical advantage.

I want to give two anecdotal examples of why I believe most people have a tendency to ignore danger cues. The first one involves one of the firearms instructors I have taught several classes with. This is a guy who has spent thousands of hours on the firing range and has heard hundreds of thousands gunshots. During a federal task force arrest within a quarter-mile from his home, shots were fired at the felony suspect. He heard the shots but admits that the first thing he thought was that they were fireworks. It was only later when he saw the incident on the news did he realize that what he actually heard was a gunfight.

The second story was told to me by a former supervisor and firearms instructor of mine. This guy was a martial artist, defensive tactics and firearms instructor, use of force specialist, experienced police officer, and son of a police officer. He freely told this story to me and other students to illustrate the importance of awareness, listening to observations and danger cues, and not rationalizing what you see and hear.

He was watching the old movie Scream years ago with his dad. They had rented the movie from a Blockbuster Video store (As you can tell this is an old story). He remembers having to return the video by midnight. So, at about ten minutes until midnight, they hurried to Blockbuster to return the movie. As they pulled up to the store, he remembered seeing only a couple of vehicles in the parking lot. One of them was still running, parked up front but not in a parking space. In fact, this vehicle was parallel to the sidewalk, although the parking spots ran perpendicular to the curb. It was crossed over a couple of spots, and he remembered thinking to himself that it must be someone picking up an employee who was about ready to get off work. As he and his dad parked and began to walk into the store, they saw a couple of guys inside near the counter wearing masks. At this point, you are probably realizing what was taking place in front of them. What did they think? Hmmm, they must be wearing masks as a promotion for the movie Scream! It was only as the guys were running out of the store with cash and guns did they realize that they had arrived at a robbery scene as it was taking place!

Many people hear that story and say no way they wouldn't have realized what was happening. Quite frankly, I do not believe most of them. Do not get me wrong, the warning signs were there, but rationalized away. I believe that is the tendency that most of us have. We do not want to see or be a part of horrible things. It is as if our mind tries to block it out like it is not happening. Knowing this and recognizing this will help take your overall mental awareness to the next level, and may just help save your life.

Both of these stories involved not just cops, but extremely good ones. Both of them are willing to admit and share those stories so others can learn from them. I personally have gained a lot of value and insight from them. Furthermore, when I teach this concept in my classes, I am amazed at how many students over the years have been willing to share their own stories with me about how they too failed to correctly perceive incidents they had witnessed.

Now that we have addressed awareness and the importance of paying attention to danger cues, the next element of being mentally prepared involves what is known as mental rehearsal. This is a critical concept that has been used successfully for decades. This is the idea that mentally practicing for potential incidents before they occur will actually help you to perform successfully when a similar incident occurs. There have been many books written on this topic, and it is a worthy investment to study the positive effects of this further.

Asking yourself what you would do if someone tried to attack you is part of this mental preparation. Mentally rehearsing scenarios where you react quickly and appropriately to danger will have a positive effect on your ability to perform under stress and increase your likelihood of success. As the saying goes in times of great stress "You do not resort to your highest level of education, but instead to your lowest level of training and instinct." In other words, if you do not physically and mentally prepare for worst-case scenarios before they exist, the chances of you coming up with a brilliant plan during a stressful incident are extremely low.

I remember a particular Sunday dayshift as a

patrol officer. It was a typically slow day when we got a statewide notification that a murder occurred. Further information was that the suspect got into a vehicle to which the registered owner lived in our jurisdiction. Although we thought it was a long shot, myself and another deputy positioned our patrol vehicles on the interstate entering our county and waited for the suspect's vehicle. While waiting we developed a plan. We were a few miles apart at different mile markers. If the suspect took the anticipated route, my fellow deputy would hopefully find the vehicle then get into a position behind him as they traveled toward me. I could then get into position behind them, and we could conduct a felony car stop involving guns drawn and specific verbal directions given to the suspect before taking him into custody. Based on our location, if the suspect decided to flee from us initiating a vehicle pursuit, officers from a nearby city agency would be in a position to deploy stop sticks to deflate his tires. We came up with a plan and I visualized it happening. I am sure the other deputy did the same. Neither of us had any idea for sure if we would actually spot the vehicle, or if the suspect would even take the anticipated route. But a logical, tactically sound plan was put into place and I mentally rehearsed a successful result.

When my fellow deputy called out on the

radio that he was behind the murder suspect's vehicle, my heart rate went up. Physiologically the symptoms of stress started to take effect. At that moment in time, there was no way I was going to come up with a brilliant plan. We were getting ready to stop a vehicle of a man who just shot and killed another man. This was one of the times in my career where I thought a gunfight was eminent. We conducted the stop, and it went almost exactly as I had visualized. I remember the nervous tension and the surreal feeling of that day, but I also remember the feeling of believing that I had been in this position before and I was prepared to handle it. My partner did an excellent job giving verbal directions and providing cover as I holstered my weapon and placed him into handcuffs. The suspect still had some of the victim's blood on his shoe. The deputy who found the murderer that day did an outstanding job, and I was glad to play a role in it. I credit mental rehearsal and preparation as a primary contributing factor to why that arrest was made safely and without incident.

Part of mental rehearsal involves envisioning ways to save your life even if you are not carrying your gun. Or you are carrying your gun but it is malfunctioning or out of ammunition. In several of my classes, I like to involve the class in crisis rehearsal drills by giving them a scenario and telling them they do not have a gun, but they have to defend their lives. They have no choice, they can either freeze and panic or fight back. One scenario I often use is an active killer intent on shooting and killing everyone in a coffee shop and he has blocked the door and you have no way out and no gun. At first, most of the class is usually sits there quietly without a plan and seems to give up and accept their fate. At that point, I usually ask if a gun is the only potentially lethal weapon they could possibly use. By the end of the discussion we as a class come up with multiple ideas of things that could be used as weapons in worst-case scenarios: hot cups of coffee to the face, chairs to the back professional wrestling style, pens and keys become weapons, etc. It gets to the point where we have come up with dozens of ingenious ways to stop a threat. I am usually very proud of the class at this point, but I remind them that in the heat of the moment they probably would not come up with these brilliant ideas. This drives home the importance of mental rehearsal! Like one of my fellow firearms instructors used to quote, "Treat people like a million bucks, but always have a plan to kill them." While the quote is obviously meant as a joke, from a mental preparation for worst-case scenarios standpoint, it's not without some merit.

One final conversation I want to have before

this chapter ends is in regard to a question I frequently ask in my classes. The question relates to mindset in the sense that it taps into the mindset you should have when faced by a deadly threat and you are forced to act. When you shoot, do you shoot to wound or do you shoot to kill? At this point I let the class answer and I always hear a variety of passionate responses from people who clearly believe that what they are saying is absolutely correct. "If you pull your gun, you shoot to kill." "I do not want to kill anyone so I would just shoot them in the leg."

In my opinion, the answer to the question I asked is neither one. When you shoot, you shoot to stop the threat. This is the justification for shooting, and this is the most accurate description of what you are doing and trying to accomplish. How do you most effectively stop the threat? In most cases aiming for center mass of the largest portion of the threat is the most tactically sound option. For the fully visible human assailant, this translates to the upper center portion of the chest.

Why not shoot to wound? First, handguns are not precision instruments. It is exceptionally difficult to pinpoint an exact spot on a human body using a concealed carry handgun. Now, add in the fact that it is a three dimensional, moving, thinking target, which is possibly shooting at you in less than ideal lighting conditions, and it does not take long to see why this is not realistic. Furthermore, what if you do shoot the person in the leg that is shooting at you? Will that shot stop the person from continuing to shoot? Possibly not. Finally, what if you "shoot to wound" and hit the bad guy's leg and inadvertently strike the femoral artery? He or she will bleed out in a matter of minutes in all likelihood. You can try saying "I'm sorry ladies and gentlemen of the jury but I was just shooting to wound, I didn't mean for it to kill the bad guy" and see how that works out. I think you get the idea that in actual situations, shooting to wound really is not a sound option.

So why not shoot to kill? Killing someone is an exceptionally difficult thing to do for most people. Ultimately, the reason you are justified in your use of deadly force is that you are faced with a potentially deadly threat. Your goal is to stop that threat. If you are able to successfully stop the threat, then deadly force is no longer needed. If the attacker puts you in that horrible situation, remember it was their decision to put you there, and what happens as a result of your justified use of force to stop the threat is their fault. For this reason, it is of utmost importance that you consistently train and learn about the use of force laws in your state. So as clearly stated as possible, your goal is not to kill, it is to stop the threat.

A chapter about mindset in the topic of firearms would not be complete without a discussion about the aftermath of a tragic incident. This is something that I frequently discuss with students in my classes because I do not think people put enough thought into it. A shooting, or any tragic event that life might bring you, will change you forever. It is important to understand that counseling, therapy, and other forms of healing are probably going to be needed and are perfectly viable ways to deal with the aftermath of a tragedy. Everyone responds to post-traumatic stress in their own way. It does not make you strange or weird to have a myriad of emotions following a tragedy. I am not a doctor or expert in this field by any means, but I have personally witnessed various people in the immediate aftermath of a tragedy. I have also been around people in the days and months following the event. Critical incidents, even legally justified self-defense shootings, will most likely have long-lasting effects on victims, survivors, witnesses, and first-responders.

To recap this chapter, mindset and awareness are absolutely critical for gaining the tactical advantage and being prepared to not just survive but win a gunfight. You have to believe in carrying concealed in order to do it, you have to carry for the right reasons. You have to look at, listen to, and be aware of your surroundings. You have to be curious and resist the urge to rationalize away your suspicions. You have to mentally rehearse positive outcomes to potentially bad situations. These are all crucial aspects of developing your ability to stop a potentially lethal threat. If you make a practice of doing these things, you will develop the mental edge that may someday save your life or another innocent person's life.

Chapter 5 – The Fundamentals of Marksmanship

During the first morning of the first firearms instructor school I ever attended, the instructor said, "Advanced shooting is nothing more than mastery of the fundamentals." I am certain beyond any shadow of a doubt that while I was listening intently, I did not fully understand the truth and wisdom contained in that statement. Since hearing those words, I have repeated them, believed in them, lived by them, and taught them to as many of my students as possible.

I am not sure that "mastery" is really an attainable level in any endeavor. Rather it is the constant goal that you strive for, similar to perfection. But what I have become increasingly sure of, is that the path to both mastery and perfection is found in the fundamentals. If you can picture the best in the world at any specific skill or craft, you can see this concept in action. The best golfers in the world are not swinging their clubs in some magical way different from the other golfers. The best basketball players in the world are not shooting the ball in some advanced, secret fashion. The best people at any single thing in the world have one important commonality. They have practiced the fundamentals more times than virtually anyone else. They have "mastered" and continue to "master" the basics. I believe that the "secret" to mastering your handgun skills, lies in the pursuit of perfection of the fundamentals.

When it comes to the fundamentals of marksmanship, I have focused on the following seven throughout the years: grip, stance, sight picture, sight alignment, trigger control, breathing, and follow-through. This chapter will be dedicated to describing each of these fundamentals, the most essential components to becoming proficient at them, and the most common mistakes I have seen shooters make throughout the years.

The first fundamental I will focus on is the grip. When it comes to a semi-automatic pistol, the primary purpose of your grip is to control the recoil of the gun. The amount of recoil (push back of the gun after the shot sometimes referred to as "kick") will vary depending on the size of the gun and the caliber of the round. As the caliber gets larger, so too does the amount of recoil. As the handgun gets smaller, this also increases the amount of recoil. Having an efficient grip to control the recoil is important for two reasons. First, controlling your gun will allow you to take more than one shot quickly and accurately. It is obvious why this is essential. Second, a bad grip can actually disrupt the cycle of operation of the pistol, which can cause it to malfunction. A malfunction during a gunfight, which I will address in great detail in a later chapter, can only be described as a worst-case scenario.

So to keep it simple, the following points are what I consider to be the most essential details when it comes to gripping a semi-automatic pistol. First, your shooting hand should be as high as possible on the back strap of the gun. Second, both your shooting hand and support hand should make as much contact with the gun as possible. Finally, your grip should be firm. It should not be so loose that there is excess movement in the gun, and it should not be so tight that fatigue quickly becomes a factor.

My final thought on the grip is that to an extent, it is unique to the shooter. All of us have different hand sizes and shapes and strengths. For me personally, I like a grip with both thumbs on the same side of the gun pressing straight forward toward my target. This locks out my wrists and orients my shooting posture toward my target. You will hear all sorts of different formulas from people claiming that sixty of your grip percent pressure should come from one hand while forty percent comes from the other hand or some other variation of that formula. I don't think we can accurately tell exactly how much pressure we are using, but even more importantly I don't think it matters. What matters is that the grip stabilizes the gun and controls the recoil while being uniquely your own.

Take some time to find a comfortable yet operational grip with your handgun of choice. Once you find it, make it your grip every time. In other words, the second you touch gun your gun you should grip it the exact same way you do when you shoot it. This is tactically sound, as well the most time-efficient way to operate. If you take additional time to adjust your grip as you move into position to fire, you are wasting time. If there is one thing you do not want to waste during a gunfight, I would suggest time would be right there in the conversation.

Up until this point, I have focused on the grip with respect to a semi-automatic pistol and not a revolver. The principles are similar with one important exception. I do not use a thumbs pointing forward grip when shooting a revolver. First, because depending on your hand size, forward extending thumbs might interfere with the rotation of the cylinder. For a revolver, the rotation of the cylinder is critical for the operation of the gun. Second, from a safety standpoint, if your thumbs get anywhere near or in front of the cylinder when the pistol is fired, this could result in a serious injury to your hand. So for a revolver grip, I like to have both thumbs on the same side of the gun, stacked on top of each other and folded downward.

Now that I have addressed the grip, the next shooting fundamental I want to explore is stance. The two words that I think best describe a good shooting stance are "athletic" and "combat." In terms of athleticism, your knees should be slightly bent in a stance similar to a volleyball or baseball player out in the field playing defense. In relation to combat, the weight of your body should be more on the balls of your feet as opposed to your heels. Furthermore, you should be leaning slightly forward as you would in a fight. I prefer my feet to be about shoulder-width apart and close to parallel with each other. My gun side foot is usually just slightly further toward the rear of my other foot. One of the most common mistakes I see from inexperienced shooters is standing with their gun side foot several feet behind their other foot. This does not create a stable shooting platform and makes the shooter less mobile if the need to move were to arise.

My preference in shooting stance is commonly referred to as an isosceles stance. It incorporates all of the previously mentioned principles and provides a stable shooting platform, which is the primary goal of any shooting stance. A firm grip and a stable shooting stance is the beginning of good marksmanship!

Sight picture and sight alignment are two fundamentals that go together hand in hand. The good news is the concept is extremely simple. But on the flip side, it does take dedicated repetition to put these two fundamentals together effectively to achieve positive hits on target. The first thing to understand is that properly aligned sights on a semi-automatic pistol mean that the rear sight posts (on the back of the gun) are level with the front sight post(on the front of the gun). If the front and rear sights are level with each other when the trigger is pressed and the shot breaks, then your shot should not be high or low. Aside from being level with each other, the front sight should be centered equally in between the rear sights. If the front sight is equally centered when the trigger is pressed and the shot breaks, your shot should not miss the target to the left or right. The most essential detail is understanding the relationship of the front sight to the rear sights. If the front sight is above the rear sights, the shot will go high. If the front sight is below the rear sights, the shot will go low. If the front sight is toward the right…you get the picture. As long as the sights are properly affixed to the gun, then where the front sight is when the shot breaks is where the shot will go. The concept itself is exceptionally easy to understand. Putting it into practice, well that's another thing entirely.

The concept of sight picture really is just as basic as the concept of sight alignment. Essentially, you are seeing three different distances when you shoot. You are seeing the rear sights, the front sight, and your target. Each of these things is a different distance from your eye. The human eye can see things at different distances at the same time; however, it cannot focus on more than one distance at any given time. So, we have a choice. We can focus on the rear sights, the front sight, or the target. For accurate shots, you should focus on the FRONT SIGHT with your dominant eye. This is easier said than done. I think it is a natural struggle for almost all shooters to resist the urge to focus on the target. But again, for accurate shots, it is essential for the beginner and even intermediate shooter to focus on the front sight while still seeing the rear sights and target. So to recap, front sight in focus, rear sights and target seen, but not in focus.

Before I move on to the next fundamental of marksmanship, I want to make a final point about sight alignment and sight picture. In a self-defense situation, aligning your sights and focusing on the front sight is something that I do not think can or should be done at a conscious level. I do not think it is necessary, and furthermore, I do not think it is worth the time that it would cost. In combat shooting, which statistically happens almost exclusively at relatively close ranges of fifteen feet and in, I think the best practice is to focus on your target and orient your gun toward the threat. But do not get it twisted, you are still accountable for the final resting spot of every round that comes out of your chamber!

There are other conversations about sight picture and sight alignment that are relevant and applicable to the fundamentals. For example, is it acceptable to close one eye to obtain a sight picture or do both eyes have to be open? Or what happens when you are right-handed but left eye dominant? What about night sights on the gun and shooting in low light conditions? What about laser sights? These are all questions I will answer another day. Maybe in a private lesson or in my next book!

Trigger control. I'm pretty sure I can write an entire chapter, possibly another book, on this fundamental alone. Many firearms instructors and gun enthusiasts consider this to be the most important, and most difficult, fundamental to master. Most of the time, when your shots did not go where they were intended to, the act of pressing the trigger was at least part of the reason. To understand trigger control, I oftentimes use the following visual for my students. Imagine that your gun is braced into a vice and the sights were perfectly aligned on target. Now imagine that the trigger of your gun takes five pounds of pressure to fire. With the sights perfectly aligned, and exactly five pounds of pressure applied straight to the rear of the trigger, the shot should go EXACTLY where it was intended.

We as humans are not machines that can lock in the gun perfectly still like a vice, nor can we apply exactly five pounds of pressure to the trigger straight to the rear. But, this is what we are striving for. Any movement in the gun will cause the round to slightly deviate from its intended location. Smoothly pressing the trigger to the rear while maintaining the most minimal arc of movement is the ultimate goal when it comes to trigger control.

You have probably heard people say in the past "you are jerking the trigger" or "you are anticipating the shot" when it comes to the reason that shots are hitting off target. While these are oversimplified explanations of errant shots, and most people (even some firearms instructors) do not really understand what they mean, there is some truth to these sayings that should be addressed.

The term "jerking the trigger" usually refers to pulling the trigger to the rear in an uncontrolled fashion at an increased speed. This typically results in a substantial amount of movement in the gun. The shooter may not even be aware they are moving the gun during the process of pressing the trigger. I have filmed many of my students in the process of shooting just so they could see how much their gun was moving. To avoid excessive movement, I suggest shooters think of the process of pressing the trigger as similar to a swinging pendulum. What I mean is equal pressure and speed as the trigger is being pressed. This smooth press directly to the rear of the gun will cause the least amount of movement before the shot breaks. The end result will be improved shot placement.

The term "anticipating the shot" usually refers to the shooter bracing the gun forward just before the shot breaks. The most common reason this is done is because the shooter knows the gun is going to recoil back toward them. The problem is this will almost always cause the gun to move more than intended, and the sights will no longer be aligned. The farther away the shot, the more pronounced the miss will be. When shooters make the two common errors I have just described, the missed shots typically end up low and to the opposite side of the shooter's strong hand. For example, a right-handed shooter will see their misses low and to the left, and a left-handed shooter will see their misses low and to the right.

Obtaining good trigger control is a lifetime mastery mission. But to get yourself on the correct path, it is important to remember the following things. Press the trigger straight to the rear with equal pressure throughout the process while your sights are aligned. Do not anticipate the shot. Allow round to break and trust your sight alignment, sight picture, grip, and stance to direct the shot where it needs to go and control the recoil. It sounds simple enough, but it takes consistent focused practice. Finally, like everything else firearms-related, it is a perishable skill.

If you ask anyone who is expected to perform at a high level under any amount of stress, they will tell you that breathing is an essential element of their success. Shooting is no exception. One of the most common mistakes I have seen from new shooters is holding their breath the entire time they are shooting. This has a tendency to cause them to shake and produce excess movement. This can disrupt their shooting platform, as well as cause fatigue.

Whether you are in a shooting competition,

training on the range, or in a gunfight to save your life, controlling your breathing with deep, focused breath will contribute to your success on many levels. Controlling your breathing will help lessen stress and fatigue while allowing you to minimize wasted movement. Furthermore, when you let a deep breath out, this brief moment in time is commonly referred to as your "natural respiratory pause." For me, this is an optimal time to break your shot. Reminding yourself to take deep, slow, controlled breaths while shooting will pay dividends in almost every shooting situation imaginable.

The final fundamental is follow-through. This can be described as the most appropriate and tactically sound course of action AFTER your shot breaks. The most common mistake inexperienced shooters make is to shoot a round, have their finger fly off the trigger and then put their gun down or back into their holster. This response is not the most tactical or effective order of operation. Instead, as soon as the first shot breaks the shooter should continue to keep their finger on the trigger, allow the trigger to reset for another shot (during the process of recoil) and then when they are sure they do not need to shoot another round their finger should immediately come off the trigger to an extended position above the trigger guard. Finally, the shooter should scan and assess the area around them to break the inevitable tunnel vision that has occurred during the act of shooting. Finally, the shooter should return the gun to the holster. The process I have just described is commonly referred to as follow-through. This practice does not have to be fast. I can't think of too many awards being given for the "fastest person to put their gun back in the holster." While it is not as well known or practiced as the other fundamentals, proper follow-though is equally important as the rest of them in your path to handgun mastery.

The previously described fundamentals are what I use EVERY time I shoot. The more you practice them and refine your physical and mental understanding of them, the better you become. It really is that simple. It does not matter how "advanced" your level of shooting is, the fundamentals will always be a critical element to your success. Whether you are engaging multiple targets, shooting on the move, using concealment and cover, shooting from alternative positions, shooting from a vehicle, or shooting with one hand, the fundamentals of marksmanship remain the same. You should constantly be striving to deepen your ability to perform the fundamentals efficiently and without the need to think about it. Your practice should be so focused that you are able to develop the ability to perform these seven fundamentals at a subconscious level without even having to think about them. If you are willing to do this, they will serve you very well in any shooting or self-defense situation. After all, "Advanced shooting is nothing more than mastery of the fundamentals."

Chapter 6 – Mastering the Draw

When I think of the draw stroke, two things come to mind. First, it is one of the most under practiced elements in all of shooting. Second, it is one of the most essential components of overall handgun competency. In other words, it is extremely important, yet highly ignored by a substantial amount of shooters. Whether you are a competition shooter, someone who carries for self-defense, or just a hobbyist who enjoys going to the range, there are a variety of reasons why you need a safe, efficient, and reliable draw. You might be a great shooter, but if you cannot get your gun out of the holster effectively, how useful is your skill?

You can do internet searches and find video after video of different instructors showing ways to draw your handgun. Some will call it the five-stage draw, the four-stage draw, the three-stage draw, etc. and explain why their way is the most useful and efficient. In my opinion, it does not really matter how many stages you break your draw into. I think what matters is that you put a few essential concepts into play every time you draw your gun. First, your draw should be consistent and repeatable. Second, it should be efficient with no wasted movement. Finally, you should practice it often and to a certain extent, it should be uniquely your own.

For the purposes of teaching the draw, I like to separate the draw into four distinct stages. Each stage has certain key components and reasons behind the importance of them. But while I separate the draw into four stages, when you practice, the goal should be to achieve one smooth and fluid draw in which one stage transitions seamlessly into the next. This is achieved through consistent, focused practiced. It's not something that needs to be drilled for hours on end, but five to ten minutes at a time of drawing your gun, once or twice a week, will take your skill level well above the vast majority of shooters.

The four stages of the draw I will discuss in this chapter are the following: Stage 1 grip and release, Stage 2 lock your wrist and rotate your arm, Stage 3 both hands come together, and Stage 4 a smooth level presentation toward your target. Understanding these four stages and practicing them to the extent that you can efficiently draw your gun without even thinking about it, is the beginning of mastering your unique draw. In countless classes, I have told students that masterful shooting begins and ends with an effective draw. I still believe this to be true now more than ever.

The draw begins by establishing a solid grip on your gun. How quickly you establish this grip depends on a few factors. First, where on your body you are carrying your gun? Second, what type of holster do you have? Third, what type of clothes are you wearing (heavy jacket, sweatshirt, etc.)? Finally, how often have you practiced drawing the gun from this location? For consistency purposes, I am going to describe the four-stage draw on the premise that you are carrying your gun in an outside the pants holster on your strong hand side near your hip. But do not get it twisted, the concepts in this four stage draw will carry over to virtually any holster location or shooting position you can think of. This is where taking general principles with you and applying them to your unique situation will serve you extremely well.

When you establish your grip, you should grip the gun exactly the same way you grip it when you shoot. This is critical because it will allow you to establish a good purchase of the gun decreasing the chance that you will fumble or drop it under stress. But more importantly, it is critical because if you have to adjust your grip before you shoot, you are wasting time. If there is something that you absolutely do not want to waste during a gunfight, it is time!

Part of establishing your grip also includes releasing whatever is holding the gun in the holster. This could be nothing, this could be friction, this could be a retention device that needs to be released with the thumb or trigger finger, or it could be a strap that snaps or Velcros over the gun. Whatever retention device you use to secure your gun into its holster, you should develop the skill required to release that retention device with ease and without even thinking about it.

One of the most common mistakes I have seen shooters make when initially gripping their gun is flaring their elbow out during the beginning of the draw. I call this "chicken winging," and it is not efficient for several reasons. Primarily because when you chicken wing the draw, you are not pulling the gun straight out of the holster at the most efficient upward angle. The proper way to draw is to keep your elbow as close to your body as possible. This will not only create the most efficient angle to draw the gun up and out of the holster but will also minimize the chance of exposing your arm outside of cover in a combat situation. Furthermore, in a concealed carry situation, keeping your elbow tight to your body will help to pin your shirt or jacket or any loose clothing to your body, so it does not interfere with the rest of your draw.

The final component of the grip and release stage of the draw is the correct placement of your non-shooting hand. A lot of shooters make the mistake of only moving their shooting hand toward their gun. This wastes time and is not efficient when it comes to achieving the ultimate goal of your draw, which is to establish a solid two-handed shooting grip on the most stable shooting platform possible. So when you go to draw your gun, BOTH hands should move at the exact same time. Your non-shooting hand should move directly to your upper abdomen near your shooting- hand side. It should be tight to your body and ready to assist your shooting hand with gripping the gun as soon as possible.

So to recap Stage 1 of the draw: grip the gun with your shooting grip and release the retention device in the most concise and efficient way possible without wasting movement, keep your arms and elbows close to your body, and finally both hands move at once. Practice this until it becomes second nature. Remember masterful shooting begins with a good draw. A good draw begins with a good Stage 1.

Stage 2 of the draw is lock and rotate, or

sometimes called lock and rock, or sometimes called lock and drop. Essentially the "lock" refers to your wrist. When you shoot, your wrist should be straight and locked out. If your wrist is bent or loose, it is very likely that this instability and movement in your wrist will interrupt the cycle of operation of your pistol. This can, and oftentimes does, result in a malfunction with your gun. The "rotate" or "rock" refers to the angle at which you are presenting your weapon toward your target. By rocking your arm immediately toward your target when the gun clears the holster, you are achieving two very important goals. First, you are orienting the muzzle toward your target in the quickest, most efficient way possible. Furthermore, when you rock your arm toward your target, you can begin to drive your gun forward as your eyes begin searching for the front sight.

The two most common mistakes shooters make during Stage 2 are "bowling" and "fishing" the gun. Bowling the gun refers to swinging the gun up toward your target in a similar fashion to bowling a ball down a lane. The problem with this is that it keeps the gun pointed at a downward angle during the majority of the draw, as opposed to pointed toward the intended target. Fishing the gun refers to swinging the gun toward your target in an upward fashion similar to how a fisherman casts a line into the water. The problem with this is also that the gun is pointed away from the intended target for the majority of the draw, only this time at an upward angle. When you lock your wrist and rock your gun forward toward the target, your gun is pointed at your target as soon as it possibly can be. Finally, in a close quarter combat situation, you could fire a round at your threat from the Stage 2 position. If you are bowling the gun you will fire into the ground, and if you are fishing the gun, you will fire into the air. Obviously, neither of these is ideal.

Stage 3 of the draw is when both hands come together to establish your shooting grip. This is an important part of the overall process of drawing your gun, but ultimately a very simple part of the process. I have already discussed grip in a previous chapter, so Stage 3 is simply achieving that grip. To do that, you should begin establishing your grip as close to your body as possible. I have found that when shooters rush their draw, they have a tendency to fumble with their grip as they extend their gun into their shooting position. This usually results in a sloppy and inefficient grip.

Stage 4 of the draw is a smooth and level presentation of the handgun toward the target. The most essential detail to a good Stage 4 of the draw is that you smoothly "punch" the gun out to eye level. It is inefficient to try to move your head down to your gun. With a good, firm two-handed grip you should punch the gun smoothly extending into your final shooting platform. This completes the presentation portion of the draw.

To end the process, the gun needs to be returned to the holster. As a general rule, the return to the holster does not have to be done quickly. In most situations, I would recommend slowly returning the gun to the holster in the exact reverse order of the draw. I think this is the most efficient way to return the gun to the holster. As you return the gun to the holster, it is a good idea to scan your entire immediate area in all directions around you. This process is sometimes known as "scan and assess." I think it is a good practice from a tactical standpoint in that it allows you to locate additional threats, witnesses, victims, etc. in a given situation. Also, under stress, the phenomenon known as "tunnel vision" is likely to occur. Scanning, assessing, and BREATHING as you put your gun back into the holster is an outstanding way to deal with tunnel vision.

This four-stage draw can be applied to virtually any holster configuration and from any shooting position. I've already mentioned it, but it's worth repeating. Even though I've separated the draw into four distinct stages, the draw should be smooth and there should be no discernable period between each stage. Your draw should be efficient, smooth, fluid, and uniquely your own.

There is one final essential point I want to make about drawing your gun before we move on. That is, at what point exactly does your trigger finger touch the trigger of the gun. This is an important piece of information and it is critical for shooters of all levels to understand when it is appropriate to put your finger on the trigger.

To answer this question, you first have to know why you are drawing your gun. While there is an infinite number of specific scenarios in which you might need to draw your gun, basically every scenario can fall in either one of two main categories. Either you are drawing your gun because you need to fire it as soon as possible (i.e. you are facing a deadly threat at that moment) or you are drawing you gun because you may need to use it (i.e. you heard a noise in the middle of the night and you are checking your home).

First I will discuss drawing your gun when you *may* need to use it. If this is the case, then at NO point during your draw should your trigger finger touch the trigger. Instead, your trigger finger should remain straight along the outside of the weapon above the trigger guard. Only once you have made the decision to fire and you have your gun pointed toward your target should your finger make the transition to the trigger.

Now let's talk about drawing the gun when you know you need to use it. This changes everything. In these situations, the trigger finger may go on the trigger as soon as it is safe and practical to do so. In a close-quarter combat situation, I would suggest that this would occur during Stage 2 of the draw. Once the gun has cleared the holster and you have locked your wrist and rocked your arm toward the threat, your finger may go on the trigger. In extreme close-quarter situations, you may have to actually fire your gun from the Stage 2 position to stop the threat.

As I said at the beginning of this chapter, the draw is one of the most essential components of handgun proficiency while simultaneously one of the most neglected. Practice your draw, perfect your draw, and make it a smooth, subconscious reflex that you can repeat with ease. If you do this, you will have taken the first step to be prepared for nearly any situation.

Chapter 7 – Handling Malfunctions

If you go to virtually any public shooting range and watch people shoot, chances are within a few minutes you will see a shooter experience a malfunction with their handgun. In the overwhelming majority of those situations, the following chain of events takes place: the shooter pauses for several seconds in a surprised state, the shooter presses the trigger again a couple more times, the shooter begins to look at the gun and wonder what is wrong with it, the shooter asks their buddy at the range with them if they can see what's wrong with their gun, and finally the shooter calls the range safety officer over to their shooting lane to see if they can figure out what's wrong with their gun.

While not every case is exactly like what I just described, most times at least some of those things take place. In this chapter, I will discuss the most common reasons that handguns malfunction, how to handle malfunctions with your handgun in an effective and tactical manner, and finally I will end the chapter with a discussion on reloading your gun. Primarily, because one particular malfunction requires the knowledge and ability to reload your gun effectively. Secondarily, because reloading your gun in general is an important skill to develop in your overall training program.

When I teach my students about handgun malfunctions, I usually start the session off with a simple question. I ask them, generally speaking, what is the most common reason that a gun malfunctions? To put it bluntly, when a gun goes "click" instead of "bang" what is the most common reason by far? What typically follows is a myriad of responses to include the following: bad ammunition, broken parts to the gun, gun is too dirty, etc. After I hear all of these common responses rattled off, I tell my students that the VAST majority of handgun malfunctions can be attributed to two words: shooter error. Yes, that is correct. While it is natural for virtually all of us to blame the gun for not working properly, it is most likely our own mistake that has caused the gun to malfunction. The number one reason of all time for a gun not to shoot when it is supposed to is the shooter forgetting to disengage the safety mechanism. The gun did, in fact, operate correctly, it was the shooter who did not operate the gun properly. Other extremely common shooter induced malfunctions include failure to properly feed and seat the magazine, and finally an improper grip and lockout of the shooters' wrists, which in turn disrupts the cycle of operation of the gun.

Now do not get me wrong, there are malfunctions that do occur because of bad ammunition, broken springs, extractors, etc. but these cases are the exception rather than the rule. Understanding this basic premise will automatically put you ahead of the game in terms of having fewer malfunctions in the first place.

Now, let's talk about how to handle a malfunction when it does occur. The problem with the scenario I described at the beginning of the chapter, is that if your response is to stop and look at the gun every time it malfunctions, you are in essence training yourself to respond this way. At the range, this is no big deal. In a gunfight, stopping to look at your gun could be a fatal mistake. So, to prepare yourself to handle a malfunction correctly in every situation, I recommend you develop a response that you use every time you have a malfunction.

Let me start out by describing the four most basic malfunctions that can occur with a semi-automatic pistol. They are the following: Failure to feed, failure to fire, failure to eject, and failure to extract (sometimes referred to as double feed). Without going into unnecessary amounts of the detail into what exactly each of these malfunctions is, they are pretty self-explanatory. The failure to feed means that for some reason a round did not feed into the chamber to be fired. The failure to fire means the round in the chamber did not fire even though the trigger was pressed. The failure to eject means the previous round may have come out of the chamber but did not fully eject out of the ejection port of the gun, usually interrupting the slide from returning to its normal position. The failure to extract means the previous round was not extracted from the chamber, usually resulting in the next round pressing forward against it in an attempt to feed into the chamber.

Now that you have a general understanding of the common malfunctions, you can begin to understand how to fix them. When your handgun goes click instead of bang, you should immediately address the situation. When this happens, you should tap the bottom of the magazine with the palm of your support hand, and then fully rack the slide to the rear by pulling it back toward you with your support hand. While pulling the slide back with your support hand, you should pressure the gun forward with your shooting hand. This is a process that should be trained and practiced with a qualified instructor until you can perform it reflexively.

The reason you tap the bottom of your magazine is to ensure that it is properly seated into the gun. If it is not actually seated into the gun, the next round will likely not feed into the chamber. When you tap the magazine it is best to use an open palm and apply one firm tap. One of the most common mistakes shooters make is they tap the bottom of their magazine several times as if they are "spanking" their gun. Aside from looking silly, this is an unnecessary waste of time. Once again, in terms of gunfights, time is not something that should be wasted. Finally, when you tap the bottom of the magazine, this action should be done while holding your gun up high toward the front of your face. The reason for this is twofold. First, keeping your gun up high is less movement than lowering your gun completely down to waist level in order to clear your malfunction. Second, when your gun is up in the air, so are your eyes. Having your eyes up is important so that you can pick up potential threats in your peripheral vision even while clearing the malfunction.

Once you have tapped the magazine with one firm tap to ensure it is seated, it is now time to fully rack the slide of the gun. The most important thing to remember when doing this is to do it with conviction! Racking the slide of a semi-automatic handgun is not something that should be done at half speed or half strength. If you do not rack the slide in a deliberate focused fashion, there is a good chance that you not only fail to clear the current malfunction but also make the situation worse.

The bottom line is this---when your gun does not work as intended, tap the magazine and rack the slide immediately. The tap and rack response will clear three of the four malfunctions that can occur: the failure to fire, the failure to feed, and the failure to eject. Train this until it becomes your immediate response to any malfunction.

So let's talk about the fourth malfunction. The dreaded double-feed! With a double feed, there is a round in the chamber and another round attempting to feed into the chamber at the same time. Because of this, the slide is pressing forward but not in enough of a position where the gun can function properly. Also, because of this pressure forward from the slide, it can be difficult to get the magazine out of the gun as well. Another problem that arises is that in the heat of battle or even in the stress of competition, it is difficult if not impossible to tell what type of malfunction you have. Because of this, the first thing you should do is tap and rack! In other words, 100% of the time that you have a malfunction your immediate response should be to tap and rack. This response will clear all malfunctions except the double-feed. So, if the tap and rack does not work, you move to step two: unload the gun, reload the gun. That is it. That is the key to double-feed malfunctions. You unload the gun, and you reload the gun. Because of the slight variances in the way semi-automatic guns function, it is up to you, the gun owner, to know the best way to unload your gun and reload your gun. This would include knowing exactly where the magazine release is located and how the magazine fits properly into the gun. For the typical semi-automatic handgun, the unload and reload process would include removing the magazine, racking the slide to remove any additional rounds, re-inserting the magazine, and re-chambering a round.

The entire discussion so far in this chapter has focused on clearing malfunctions that may occur with a semi-automatic pistol. But what about a revolver? That is a reasonable question and one that I will address now. Fortunately, the answer is fairly simple. First, one of the advantages to using a revolver is that malfunctions are rare. Second, it is a very simple order of operation to follow when a revolver malfunctions. First, you press the trigger again. If that does nott work, you unload the gun, and reload the gun. If it sounds like a simple concept, that is because it is. There is no reason to overcomplicate things, especially when it comes to tactics in a gunfight.

The last topic I want to explore in this chapter is reloading. There are different types of reloads to practice such as speed reloads, empty gun reloads, tactical reloads, etc., but the premise of any type of reload is that you are putting a new fully loaded magazine into your gun. With that in mind, your goal should be to do it efficiently in a smooth, fluid fashion, with minimal wasted movement.

The general consensus of a speed reload is that you release the magazine that is in your gun and let it drop to the ground. You obtain a fully loaded magazine from your pocket or magazine holder, and finally, you insert the new magazine into your gun. Just like when you clear malfunctions, your hands and eyes should be up when reloading your gun.

An empty gun reload, sometimes called an emergency reload or slide lock reload, is similar in concept. Ultimately, your gun is now empty, (usually indicated by the slide locking back to its rearmost position) and you need to put in a new magazine. The concept is virtually identical to a speed reload.

Finally a tactical reload is performing a reload

in which you keep the magazine that is in your gun on your person when you take it out of the gun, and replace it with a fully loaded magazine. Sometimes a tactical reload is referred to as a reload with retention. Simply meaning that as opposed to dropping the magazine to the ground, the shooter keeps the partially loaded magazine on them in case they need it later. Tactical reloads are meant to be performed during a lull in the action of a gunfight. In order to perform a tactical reload at the optimal time, the shooter should have sufficient time in any given situation, cover from potential threats, and distance from potential threats.

This chapter can be summarized in the following way. There are four basic malfunctions that can happen at any time: failure to feed, failure to fire, failure to eject, and failure to extract (double feed). To truly become proficient with a handgun, you have to understand that the vast majority of malfunctions are shooter induced. Because of this, knowing your weapon and performing the fundamentals are essential. If your gun does malfunction, you need to have an immediate action that you know how to do without even thinking about it or hesitating. The one I recommend is a firm tap of the magazine to ensure it is seated and a solid focused rack of the slide to make sure a round is chambered and ready to fire. If the tap and rack procedure does not clear the malfunction, then unload the gun and reload the gun. Learn and practice reloading your gun in an efficient and safe manner with minimal wasted movement. If you understand and do these things, your proficiency will be well above that of most shooters.

Chapter 8 – Training

Of all the chapters in this book, this is one of the most exciting for me. I have a passion for teaching and training and concepts for improving the quality and frequency of training always resonate with me. As a firearms student, a firearms instructor, a martial arts student, and martial arts instructor, the topic of training has always been one of my favorites. I have studied training and teaching styles in both my personal and professional life for decades. The more I learn about training and teaching and growing and improving, the more I believe in the concept of being a lifelong student.

Some people look at training as a necessary evil. Some people claim that if you are training the "right" way then you will hate every minute of it. Others think that training is something that can be done once, then after the skill is learned they can move on to new more "advanced" skills. For example, if you want to learn about a certain topic, you can take a class about it and then you have learned what you need to know. I completely disagree with both premises that training should be tough and unenjoyable to be effective, as well as that training is a one-time event.

I addressed this in Chapter 2 but it is worth recapping because it puts things into perspective very well in my opinion. If you took your son or daughter to play a sport, say baseball or softball, and the coach tells them you are going to practice one time, how effective will that be? During the practice, they will learn to throw, catch, run, hit, and learn the rules of the game. After that practice, they are only going to play games. How successful do you think they are going to be? My students, especially the ones who are parents, all nod in agreement that this would not be a successful course of action. Yet still it amazes me how many people think they can "take a class" on a topic and that will be all the knowledge and skill they will need in that particular topic.

I could literally teach the same exact class to one of my students three times, and each time without exception they would pick up additional information that did not land the first time. This is normal, and this is something that needs to be understood.

What I have found is that a lot of people desire to be very skilled at firearms. But very few people understand what it takes to become good. Simply put, they do not put in enough time training and perfecting the fundamentals of marksmanship. Instead, they practice some and buy new gear, and their skill level tends to plateau or increase at a frustratingly slow rate.

The secret to becoming good, although not really a secret at all, is to consistently practice in a determined and focused way. But what exactly does that mean and how can you do it? First and foremost training must be an enjoyable experience in my opinion. That does not mean that it does not take hard work at times. It also does not mean that there will not be good training days and bad training days. Of course, it can be tough and of course, some days will be better than others. What it means is that training is an integral part of the process of handgun mastery. Because it is so important, you have to do it consistently. What better way to make sure you do something consistently than to make it fun!

How do you make training fun? Well to some extent, that question can be answered differently from person to person. But I am going to share with you some of the tricks I have learned over the years to make training a fun, productive, experience that I look forward to every day!

First, remove all of the pressure from yourself

when training. I know that can be easier said than done, but I am telling you it is probably the single most determining factor on how much you will enjoy your training. So many of us are competitive perfectionists that put an exceptional amount of pressure on ourselves when shooting. If you happen to miss a few shots, the shooting session tends to go downhill and becomes a less than enjoyable experience. Remember this: when you practice, you are getting better! You are increasing your experience and your familiarity with the gun. So breathe, relax, and have fun when you are shooting!

Second, be creative when you train. If you do the same drills, work the same skills, fire from the same distances, at the same targets....well, you get the point. Change things up when you practice. Invent new drills. Imagine scenarios that you might be in, whether it is in a competition or in an actual self-defense situation. Shoot at different ranges. Shoot indoors and outdoors. Try different types of guns. Shoot with different people. Try shooting competitions. Play paintball. In other words, keep things fun, new, and exciting!

If you can remove the pressure from training, and keep it different and exciting, I have no doubt that training will become an enjoyable experience for you. Naturally, if it becomes enjoyable, you will do it more often. If you train more often...it is not difficult to see where I am going with all of this.

So now that we have established that training should be fun and enjoyable, we have one other element to put in place. Training should be productive and effective. In other words, if you want to be proficient with your gun, there are certain things you should involve in your training to get you there.

Dry fire practice is one of the most important aspects of effective training. And the beautiful part about it is that it costs nothing but your time! Dry fire practice is drawing and manipulating your gun without actually shooting live rounds. It can be done in almost any environment that you can find a safe direction to point your gun. You can practice your grip, stance, aligning your sights and obtaining a sight picture, pressing your trigger, breathing and even following through. Literally the only thing you cannot do in a dry fire setting is feel the shot break and feel the recoil of the gun. And now with virtual simulator products, you can even do that! But again it's amazing how much you can actually practice and even more importantly how much you can improve by dry firing your weapon. I would go as far as to say that dry firing is the single most important thing you can do to become an amazing shooter. The amount of dry fire practice you do can easily be the difference between being a moderate shooter and a great shooter. I can tell you definitively that the best shooters in the world dry fire more than they actually live fire. By a lot. Think about that. One final note about dry firing: NEVER have live ammunition in the room when you are dry firing. Remember, without proper consideration of firearms safety, nothing else matters!

Another way to make your training more effective is to create and maintain a training log. It can be extremely detailed, or it can be fairly generic, but I have found that training logs can be extremely effective in not only measuring your progress in times and scores on courses and drills, but it can also be a great motivator to train and push yourself to improve. Training logs can monitor your frequency and your approximate round counts. But most importantly, training logs can put you in competition with your best rival of all time: yourself! Try doing a training log for three months and monitor your progress. I am certain you will be happy with the results.

Find opportunities to train that are both scheduled and unscheduled. For example, if you carry concealed, every time you put your gun and holster on do a few draws before you secure your weapon. A few draws a day turns into several draws a week, which in turn leads to hundreds of practice repetitions over the course of several months. The time is going to pass anyway, so you might as well keep getting better as it does!

I would be remiss if I did not include in this chapter *what* you should train. While this is not an exhaustive list, the following things belong in your training program! Constant, continuous, lifelong review of the cardinal rules of firearms safety, dry fire practice of the seven fundamentals of marksmanship, drawing your weapon from your holster or bag, clearing malfunctions, engaging multiple targets, shooting at different distances, shooting in less than ideal lighting conditions, shooting and moving, and shooting from different positions (squatting, kneeling, prone, etc.).

When it comes to training, I think even the best among us should be willing to be students. Even as a firearms instructor, I love taking various firearms classes. There are many ways to do things and there is a lot of information out there! Sign up for classes as part of your training. Unfortunately, some of them will be good, and some of them will be bad. It's just the reality of the firearms world. As a teacher, I have lived, believed, and practiced the tenant that there are no bad students, only bad teachers. So if the class was bad, it was not your fault. But even in classes that are not good, something can be learned. Always look for the lesson to be learned in every experience, even if the lesson simply is what not to do.

I wanted to keep this chapter short on purpose because the reality is I can, and probably will, write an entire other book solely on training, learning, and practicing. For now, I think the essential points are that training can and should be a fun and pressure-free experience that you look forward to. You should be creative when you train, and you should do it often. The best shooters in the world, as well as the best teachers in the world, will always be perennial students.

Chapter 9 – Defensive Tactics

Some of my students throughout the years have wanted to shoot only for the fun of the hobby. But I would say the vast majority at least in part wanted to learn the fundamentals of handgun operation for purposes of self or home defense. One of my most popular classes through the years has been my tactical handgun course.

While training and exploring the topic of tactical handgun principles there are two things to remember that are more important than everything else. First, the four cardinal rules of firearms safety ALWAYS apply. Second, the fundamentals of marksmanship ALWAYS come with you. If you can remember and practice those two concepts, you will be ready to successfully learn handgun tactics.

For the remainder of this chapter, I will discuss and explain some of the most important tactical handgun concepts that I have trained and taught over the years.

I think good tactics always start with the proper mindset. Buzzwords like "situational awareness" get thrown around and accepted but I do not think they always get truly understood. To put it simply, a brief but purposeful analysis of your environment is the beginning of gaining the tactical edge. Where are the high points? Where are the blind spots? Where are the escape routes? Where are the open areas? Where are the points of cover and/or concealment? This is not difficult to do, and with focused practice, it can become something you do almost second nature. As discussed previously, add being acutely aware of people in the environment and you are starting to put yourself at an advantage to act to defend yourself or others if you needed to. This is how you make yourself a very difficult target.

Statistically speaking, the overwhelming majority of deadly shootings happen in very close quarters. Simply put, most gunfights occur between people who are in very close proximity to each other. Knowing this, in order to gain the tactical advantage, you should include draw and fire from close quarter drills, movement and angling drills, and one-handed shooting drills into your self-defense training.

Understanding the terms "cover" and "concealment" is also an integral component of having sound tactics. Cover is an object, wall, or other entity capable of not only concealing your location but also providing protection from incoming bullets. Examples of cover include large brick walls, engine compartments of vehicles, etc. Concealment is capable of hiding you from a threat, but not capable of stopping incoming bullets. Examples of concealment include dry wall, car doors, trees, etc. Knowing the difference between cover and concealment is critical to planning escape routes or getting to a position of safety to call for help.

In addition to occurring in extremely close quarters, a large percentage of deadly force encounters occur in less than ideal light conditions. For this reason, part of your tactical handgun training should include shooting, moving, loading and unloading your gun, and clearing malfunctions while using a flashlight. Do this first in a dry setting and make sure you become proficient to the point that you can achieve those tasks without having to think about them.

In all of my tactical courses, I make sure to emphasize the following point. Not all self-defense scenarios require the use of deadly force. In other words, if you think carrying a gun is the only thing you need to do to protect yourself, you are missing out on the big picture. If you carry a gun and shoot but have zero knowledge of empty-hand self-defense techniques, you are not completely preparing yourself to defend against an attack. Through the last several years I found that there are so many parallels between training in firearms and martial arts. The two disciplines go together hand in hand, and I could make a substantial argument that they are not different disciplines at all.

When practicing to become more tactically sound, it is always a good idea to add a communication element to your training drills. This would be especially true if you train with friends or family. As I frequently tell my students, one of the most important things to have in a life and death situation is effective communication. Simultaneously, one of the most difficult things to achieve in a life and death situation is effective communication. I have seen communication successes and communication breakdowns in countless simulated and real-life scenarios. The importance of effective communication cannot be overstated. To keep it simple, always remember the following two things. First, to communicate effectively in stressful situations, speak slowly, loudly, and clearly. Second, assume a message has not been received until you get an acknowledgment from the intended receiver of the message.

The next two tactical tips will come straight

from one of my training tips of the day I wrote for my company page at Top Firearms Instruction:

The next time you shoot, don't just put holes in paper. Mentally put yourself in scenarios in which you are stopping a deadly threat. Think about what you would say, consider movement, concealment, and cover options. Hold yourself accountable for ANY missed shots. Shoot as quickly and efficiently as you can accurately put positive hits on target. Think about controlling your breathing and scanning your environment. The more you train like this, the more prepared you will be in worse case scenarios.

Occasionally practice one-handed shooting. The benefit for self-defense is that one-handed shooting may become necessary if you are holding a flashlight, if your other arm is wounded, or if you are in a close quarter fight and one hand is engaged in the fight. The benefit for overall marksmanship is that it helps you understand the importance of a proper grip and a locked wrist for recoil control.

Handgun tactics is a fascinating topic. Experts of all sorts will agree and disagree about the best tactics in this scenario or that scenario, but the reality is different tactics work in different situations for different people. What might work one day, might not work another day. What might work against one adversary, might not work against another. In this chapter, I briefly summarized some of the more important themes and concepts that I have seen over the years when it comes to tactics. They are meant to be explored and further developed on your own. The best advice I can give you is to prepare yourself mentally and physically, and all things being equal, go with the simplest option. Train hard and always be safe!

Conclusion

In this book, I have discussed some of the most important concepts I have learned over the years about fundamental handgun mastery. Firearms Safety and the Fundamentals of Marksmanship have always been, and will always be the most important aspects. Without either of them, I do not believe true handgun mastery is possible. Once you believe and understand this, then you can apply the training and mindset principles outlined in previous chapters. Once you have combined all of that together, there is no limit to what you can achieve in terms of handgun proficiency.

I realize that a substantial portion of this book has been concept-based, and not particularly composed of specific instructional steps. This was by design. My intention was to expand your knowledge and encourage thinking and self-discovery of this topic. The reason this is so important is that you can find twenty different firearms "gurus" that will tell you twenty different ways to do things. Many of them will arrogantly claim their way is the best. I am not saying that all firearms instructors are arrogant, or that there isn't a lot of outstanding information out there. But I have discovered throughout the years, that for all of the great information there is just as much bad, untested, and sometimes deceptively dangerous information out there. Just go to any internet chat room related to firearms and it won't take you long to see my point.

Oftentimes it is up to the individual gun owner to apply their own filter to what information is relevant, effective, and will work for them. Because of this, I wanted this book to improve your knowledge conceptually so that you can apply your own principles to your training and understanding of firearms. Furthermore, whether you are new to firearms, or an experienced shooter, I want to genuinely thank you for being willing to read and expand your knowledge on this topic. I am truly humbled and thankful to have reached and connected with so many of you throughout the years and I plan to continue this journey.

Moving forward, if you follow the principles laid out in this book, I have no doubt you will continue to learn and improve at an incredible rate. Ultimately that was my primary goal in writing this book. I have had the unique and fortunate pleasure of teaching and learning from some of the most amazing people in the world over the years. I wanted to share some of the most important things I have learned. Furthermore, I wanted to improve your knowledge and understanding so that not only can you enjoy this amazing hobby, but also so you can develop the physical and mental skills to protect you and your friends and family if the need were ever to arise. To that extent, I hope I have helped you on your path to handgun mastery.

Please subscribe to my YouTube channel Top Firearms Instruction, as I will publish training and range videos to compliment this book. Also, follow me on Facebook at Top Firearms Instruction for Training Tips of the Day and Range Drills of the Week. Finally, please leave a review of *Fundamental Handgun Mastery* on Amazon so more potential readers will explore this topic!

See you at the range. Train hard and be safe my friends!

About the Author

Tyson Kilbey is a teacher and lifelong student. At the time of the most recent publication, he has 18 years of law enforcement experience and has worked the ranks of Deputy, Master Deputy, Sergeant, and Lieutenant. Throughout his career he has worked in detention, patrol, training, SWAT, accident investigation, and has been a member of his agency's competition shooting team. He has a Bachelor of Science in Justice Studies from Fort Hays State University, and has been studying various martial arts for twenty years. He has taught thousands of law enforcement officers across the Midwest in both firearms and self-defense courses as well thousands of civilians from all walks of life through his company Top Firearms Instruction. He has created law enforcement training programs as well as community programs for gun safety and bully prevention for children. Tyson is a certified instructor with the world famous Gracie Jiu Jitsu Academy and a Master Instructor with the Carotid Restraint Institute. He has successfully competed in several shooting matches over the last decade, and served as range safety officer and match director for several shooting competitions across the Midwest.

Printed in Great Britain
by Amazon

75101672R00077